In memory of my father:

like Jesus even in the last moment

Acknowledgments

To my wife, Angela: thank you for your support and for challenging me to focus on my passions. Your encouragement, honesty, and faith have been foundational to this project.

To my children, Dylan, Nora, Evan, and Hannah: thank you for your patience and understanding as I spent hyper-focused mornings and evenings immersed in this work. You are constant reminders of God's grace and joy in my life.

To Pastors Laurel Bunker and Drew Johnson: thank you for unknowingly sparking a creative idea that had been sitting dormant, waiting to be tapped. Your leadership and insight planted seeds that have grown into this work.

To my friends and mentors: thank you for walking alongside me in this journey of faith. You have not only encouraged me to write but also shown me what it means to live like Jesus.

To you, the reader: thank you for engaging with this devotional. Your commitment to reflecting, learning, and living out these challenges inspires me to keep pressing on. May this journey draw you closer to Jesus and help you reflect His light in the world.

Table of Contents

Introduction

Day 1: Grow Like Jesus

Day 2: Serve Like Jesus

Day 3: Include Like Jesus

Day 4: Heal Like Jesus

Day 5: Teach Like Jesus

Day 6: Remember Like Jesus

Day 7: Retreat Like Jesus

Day 8: Silent Like Jesus

Day 9: Talk Like Jesus

Day 10: Personal Reflection

Day 11: Impartial Like Jesus

Day 12: Witness Like Jesus

Day 13: Comfortable Like Jesus

Day 14: Obey Like Jesus

Day 15: Celebrate Like Jesus

Day 16: Work Like Jesus

Day 17: Eat Like Jesus

Day 18: Sleep Like Jesus

Day 19: Wait Like Jesus

Day 20: Personal Reflection

Day 21: Fight Like Jesus

Day 22: Ask Like Jesus

Day 23: Cry Like Jesus

Day 24: Walk Like Jesus

Day 25: Worship Like Jesus

Day 26: Invest Like Jesus

Day 27: Cook Like Jesus

Day 28: See Like Jesus

Day 29: Share Like Jesus

Day 30: Reflection

Day 31: Pray Like Jesus

Day 32: Linger Like Jesus

Day 33: Focus Like Jesus

Day 34: Battle Like Jesus

Day 35: Make Room Like Jesus

Day 36: Imagine Like Jesus

Day 37: Play Like Jesus

Day 38: Unafraid Like Jesus

Day 39: Forgive Like Jesus

Day 40: Overcome Like Jesus

The Why and the Way

Striving to be like Jesus has been part of the Christian tradition since its inception. Every generation of Christ-followers has received encouragement to let their attitudes mirror His, building on the early Christian mandate that our minds should be shaped by Christ's mindset. The Apostle Paul affirmed this idea, urging others to follow him as he followed after Christ.

My own journey was marked by a season of idealism, inspired by the familiar question, *"What would Jesus do?"* (WWJD). Emulating Jesus' life, with all its moral and ethical resonance, is admirable and worthwhile—and it's transformative. It can deepen our character, help us love more fully, and guide us in navigating the complexities of life.

But there's more here than ethical improvement. Being like Jesus isn't just about doing good; it's also a pathway to being *with* Him. Modeling our lives after Jesus fosters a relational connection that studying His words alone cannot. When we learn to live as He lived—even if applied imperfectly to our own context—we find ourselves drawn closer to Him. To be like Jesus is to dwell with Jesus.

Living like Jesus can at times feel daunting and intangible. As we encounter His miracles and compassion, we might tie much of what He did to His divinity, forgetting that He also entered into our human experience. He came to stand where we stand, to walk where we walk, and to feel what we feel. It's in the ordinary, tangible aspects of His life—His work, His rest, His relationships—that we find the fullest point of connection. By looking at how Jesus navigated daily life, we learn that imitating Him is not only possible but profoundly meaningful.

Why Model Our Lives After Jesus?

Jesus provides a divine yet human model of compassion, humility, and purpose. His life can shape ours with depth and grace. This isn't about earning salvation or proving worthiness—Jesus Himself is the mode of access to God's promises.

The attempt to model our lives after Jesus is not an attempt to earn anything or prove our value; it is an attempt to express the value and worth we already have in Christ. For those exploring faith, Jesus' example brings clarity and may spark the desire to know Him more intimately. For those already following, it's a call to let His life refine and guide us.

We do not transform ourselves alone. The Spirit draws us, and Jesus' death and resurrection secure our relationship with God. Responding to His love, rather than striving for perfection, is what ultimately matters.

Why 40 Days?

The number 40 carries deep significance throughout Scripture. It appears in the story of Noah—40 days of de-creation followed by renewal. It symbolizes trust, provision, and restoration, reflecting rightness between humanity, God, and creation. The number 40 and its significance continue throughout God's story—from Moses to the nation of Israel, from Elijah to even the city of Nineveh.

Jesus Himself spent 40 days in the wilderness, seeking clarity and communion with His Father. This devotional journey mirrors that intensity, inviting you into a purposeful exploration of Jesus' life. These 40 days of devotional entries and reflections are meant to do more than merely build habits. They are written so that you might engage wholeheartedly in your spiritual growth.

My hope is that you will commit to 40 days of seeking clarity and communion with God through attempting to mirror Jesus in your actions.

How This Devotional is Structured

This journal is flexible and personal. Each day begins with a narrative reflection on Jesus' life and a brief commentary connecting His world to ours. Entries are followed by white space for you to write, sketch, pray, or explore connected Scriptures. These pages begin with a few reflective questions to help prompt some thoughts and reflection.

Every 10 days the entries are designed to help you *imagine* with Scripture—to fill in the blanks and margins of the narrative. Life happens in the margins, and Scripture invites us to experience our humanness in those spaces. Be curious. Ask reflective questions about environments and encounters in Jesus' life that are not so different from our own.

Intentionally Non-linear

Entries are intentionally not in chronological order. This disruption is by design. Life rarely unfolds in a straight line, and neither does growth. Our spiritual pathways are nonlinear—marked by moments of challenge, discovery, and re-discovery. This format mirrors the way we experience and reflect on our own lives, jumping between memories, lessons, and inspirations. Relationships grow through shared stories that emerge in no particular order.

There is a checklist of the entries in chronological order that can be found in the appendix (if you just find it too unsettling) . I do encourage you to embrace the format as it is, letting it disrupt familiar patterns and draw you into fresh engagement.

To follow Jesus is not about completing a timeline of spiritual behaviors. It's about walking in real time, your time, alongside Him. As you work through each story and reflection, remember that part of working out your salvation is discovering how to live like Jesus in your time and context—a world very different from His.

May these reflections draw you deeper into the story of Jesus. May you discover the abundance of His compassion, the clarity of His calling, and the joy of being with Him. May His life inspire and shape your own, not just for these 40 days but for a lifetime of walking in step with Him.

Like Jesus Prayer

Father,
Shape my heart to love like Jesus,
Open my eyes to see like Jesus,
Strengthen my hands to serve like Jesus,
And guide my steps to walk with Jesus.
Amen.

Day 1 — Luke 2:41-45

Grow Like Jesus

Seeking and Finding

Every spring, Jerusalem buzzed with life for the Passover festival. Narrow streets brimmed with travelers, the air alive with the scents of festival food and friendly banter. Among these pilgrims was a young Jesus and His family, joining a sacred tradition that connected them to their faith, community, and ancestors.

When the week-long festival ended, Mary and Joseph set out for home, assuming Jesus was somewhere in the familiar crowd of relatives and friends. By evening, He was nowhere to be found. Their hearts pounded as they retraced their steps all the way back to Jerusalem.

Three days of frantic searching finally led them to the temple. Jesus was seated among the teachers, listening, asking questions, and astonishing everyone with His understanding. Exhausted and exasperated, Mary asked, *"Son, why have You treated us like this? We've been anxiously searching for You!"*

Jesus' response was gentle and curious: *"Why were you looking for Me? Didn't you know I had to be in My Father's house?"* The meaning of His words eluded them, and hinted at a deepening wisdom. He returned home with Mary and Joseph to Nazareth—a politically and economically insignificant town. There, in the quiet rhythms of daily life, Jesus grew in his understanding of God and people, he matured and gained the favor of God and people.

The Hidden Path to Maturity

Jesus was a child prodigy, capturing the attention of religious leaders at a young age. His uniqueness would have granted him access to the up-in-coming religious scholars of the day. He could have basked in the admiration of those who recognized His potential. Instead, He chose to return home—to a humble community, in an unremarkable place with simple and faithful relationships.

In Nazareth, Jesus embraced growth on God's terms—not the world's terms. Like Moses in the wilderness, He matured and developed in obscurity. The Gospel writer's inclusion of this episode reminds us that true formation often happens away from the spotlight, in places and relationships we might overlook. Jesus' path to maturity defied expectations, teaching us that genuine growth rarely aligns with worldly measures of prestige.

How/Now

Embrace Community: Reflect on who surrounds you—family, neighbors, mentors, friends. What can you learn from them, regardless of their status or education?

Find Lessons in the Everyday: Look for God's hand in your daily routines. Small, ordinary moments can be formative.

Pursue Balance: Growth is multifaceted. Consider practical steps to nurture your intellect, health, spiritual depth, and relationships this week.

What opportunities for growth might you be overlooking in your daily life?

Who can help you grow, and how might you engage with them intentionally this week?

What is one step you can take toward the growth God is calling you to?

Proverbs 1:5 | Philippians 1:9-11 | 1 Samuel 16:7

Day 2	Matthew 20:26

Serve Like Jesus

The Basin and the Towel

The night before His arrest, Jesus yet again surprised his disciples with his actions. Jesus took a basin of water, wrapped a towel around His waist, and knelt to wash their dusty and dirty feet. These were His closest friends, the ones who had shared His meals, followed Him through crowded villages, and still struggled to understand His mission. He chose to serve them through an unglamorous, common—menial "chore." The act nearly offended the disciples. They felt this was beneath their teacher and master—and certainly beneath them, since none had volunteered for the task themselves.

This was precisely the point. Jesus didn't set out to impress them with miracles or profound words about humility. He showed them what love looks like when it stoops to the level of ordinary. By doing this lowly, everyday task, Jesus revealed that serving isn't reserved for special occasions or grand gestures. It's woven into the very fabric of daily relationships, an outflow of genuine care that meets practical needs right where they exist.

Greatness Hides in the Ordinary

We often think serving God means looking for big opportunities—a faraway relief trip, a major volunteer role, or a remarkable act of kindness. Jesus' example reminds us that service often happens in spaces we overlook because they seem too small, messy, or routine. Our love made known through serving is tested among those who see our everyday imperfections—those who feel the brunt of our frustrations or disappointments. This is when *Jesus-like* serving comes to life, when we honor those nearest to us by meeting their needs, even if it's messy, inconvenient, or unacknowledged.

Jesus invites us to adopt an attitude that places others' needs above our pride or convenience. This is humility in action: seeing what needs to be done and doing it, even if it's not our "job," even if it feels beneath us. It's about caring enough to meet someone right where they are, in the ordinary grit and grind of life.

How Now?

Look for the Unnoticed Task: Pay attention to the everyday opportunities to serve—like tidying a shared space, running an errand, or stepping into a role no one else wants.

Embrace the Ordinary: Don't dismiss acts of service because they seem too trivial. Small actions can speak louder than well-intentioned but distant gestures.

Set Pride Aside: If something feels "beneath you," consider that an invitation to serve. True greatness isn't about status; it's about loving others through humble action.

Where do you encounter simple needs you've been ignoring?

How might embracing everyday acts of service transform your closest relationships?

What steps help you set aside pride and serve with humble care?

Philippians 2:3-4 | Galatians 5:13 | Acts 9:36

Day 3   Luke 10:38-42

Include Like Jesus

When Inclusion Defies Tradition

In a small village, Jesus entered the home of two sisters, Mary and Martha. Traditionally, to sit at the teacher's feet and learn Scripture was reserved for men. Women were expected to tend to domestic tasks and remain in the background. Martha busied herself with serving, anxious to provide the proper hospitality. Mary, however, defied convention- quietly taking a seat among the disciples, listening intently.

The tension in the room mounted as Martha urged Jesus to send her back to the kitchen. Surely He would restore the norm, uphold the cultural boundaries but instead, Jesus affirmed Mary's choice. She had chosen what was better. He overturned tradition with a simple affirmation, revealing that in God's kingdom, every person is invited to learn, grow, and belong. Jesus signaled that God's kingdom would embrace those previously excluded.

Opening the Door for Everyone

To include like Jesus is to tear down the barriers that keep people from full participation in the life God intends. Jesus consistently welcomed those society had pushed aside: women, foreigners, the poor, and the chronically ill. The movement He started still calls us outward, toward those who have yet to encounter God's love.

The world has its hierarchies and unspoken rules about who belongs where. Jesus modeled a radical openness—giving Mary permission to learn, to question, to sit in the seat of a disciple. This wasn't a token gesture; it was a deliberate overturning of expectations, showing that in God's kingdom, worth is rarely measured by the same standards of the societies and systems around us.

Today, we carry on this legacy of inclusion. We look beyond labels and differences, inviting everyone into conversation, community, and service. When we include this way, we join an ever-expanding movement that ensures everyone has the space to know and grow in Christ's love.

How Now?

Identify Those on the Margins: Consider who in your community or church might feel overlooked or out of place. How can you create space for their voice and presence?

Challenge Cultural Norms: Don't settle for "the way things have always been." Ask how you can follow Jesus' example by making room for those traditionally excluded.

Elevate Others' Gifts: Affirm and appreciate the insights, leadership, and contributions of people who may not fit societal expectations.

Orient Outward: Keep the focus on those who have yet to experience God's love. Seek ways to invite and include them, demonstrating that the kingdom is open to all.

Who in your life might feel like they don't have a seat at the table? How can you invite them in?

What social norms need challenging so more people can encounter God's love through you and your community?

How might embracing an outward focus in your relationships help others find their place in God's story?

Galatians 3:28 | James 2:1–4 | Proverbs 22:2

Day 4   Mark 5:1–20

Heal Like Jesus

Restored to Community

A wild man lived among the tombs—isolated, tormented, and feared. People tried restraining him with chains, but he tore them apart. No one could help. He endured suffering alone, crying out day and night in a realm of death and decay.

Then Jesus stepped ashore. Faced with a man ravaged by spiritual oppression and cultural isolation. Jesus didn't recoil. With calm authority and profound compassion, Jesus freed the man from the grip of torment and evil. The healing didn't stop there. Once calm and in his right mind, the man begged to follow Jesus, hoping for a new start far from the place of his shame. But Jesus did something unexpected: He sent him back to his own people, saying "Go home and tell your story."

Jesus restored not only his mind and body but his place in the community. This man would no longer be defined by his affliction. Instead, he would become a living testimony of mercy and renewal among those who once avoided and feared him. Healing, in this moment, meant reintegration— the man back into the human family, restoring his dignity and voice.

Beyond Symptoms

When we think of healing, we often imagine the instant reversal of physical symptoms. But Jesus' example shows that true healing is holistic. It involves seeing beyond the affliction—be it mental illness, addiction, trauma, or social alienation—and restoring the person's identity, relationships, and humanity.

We may not cast out demons, but we can follow Jesus' pattern of healing by acknowledging suffering, showing compassion, and fostering environments where people can be heard and accepted. For those burdened by stigmatizing conditions or crushing hardships, healing might mean helping them reconnect with their community, rewrite their narrative, and find belonging. Like Jesus, we're invited not only to recognize their struggles but to envision the wholeness God desires for them.

How Now?

See the Whole Person: Don't reduce others to their struggles or symptoms. Look for their unique story and worth beneath the pain.

Extend Compassion and Presence: Simply showing up, listening, and caring is itself a healing balm. Be a safe place for someone to share their hurt.

Restore Relationships: Consider how you can help someone reconnect with family, friends, or supportive communities. Healing often involves rebuilding broken ties.

Champion Their Story: Encourage those who've found hope or healing to share their journey. Their testimony can break down stigma and inspire others toward wholeness.

Who in your life might be marginalized or isolated due to their struggles?

In what ways can you be part of someone's process of restoration—relationally, emotionally, or spiritually?

How does viewing healing as a holistic process change your perspective on what it means to "help" someone in need?

Psalm 147:3 | 2 Samuel 9:7

Day 5   Matthew 13:34-35

Teach Like Jesus

Story Shifts Perspective

A lawyer approached Jesus with a question—one designed to test Him: "What must I do to inherit eternal life?" The lawyer knew the commandments well, and recited them to Jesus. Still he pressed further, wanting to prove himself right. "Who is my neighbor?" He asked. This could have descended into endless debate, dissecting legal definitions. Instead, Jesus turned to imagination and empathy. He told a story.

A man traveling from Jerusalem to Jericho falls into the hands of robbers and is left half-dead. Two respected religious figures pass by without helping. Then a Samaritan—an outsider, despised by the Jews—sees the victim's need and responds with compassion and care. By painting this vivid scene, Jesus breaks biases and reveals that true neighbors aren't defined by status or familiarity. Love crosses boundaries that logic and tradition can't easily breach.

Stirring Hearts and Minds

When we think of teaching, of helping others learn, we might picture lectures, bullet points, or data. Jesus leaned on story to help others learn. He crafted word-pictures that touched both heart and mind. Stories invite listeners to step into another's world and wrestle with choices from fresh angles. Through narrative, Jesus helped people transcend prejudice, outgrow intellectual barriers, and discover truths that might remain hidden in a purely academic debate.

This approach isn't about avoiding complexity. It's about using creativity to reach deeper levels of understanding. Stories linger, they prompt us to ask questions long after a conversation ends. If we want to teach like Jesus, we can learn from His willingness to engage the imagination—communicating values through narratives that resonate beyond the walls of argument.

How Now?

Embrace Storytelling: Instead of relying on facts and arguments, consider how a simple narrative can illuminate a concept.

Observe the World: Look for everyday moments—small kindnesses, resolved conflicts, personal struggles—to form the raw material for meaningful stories.

Spark the Imagination: Embrace creativity. Experiment with analogies, metaphors, and parables that help listeners connect the dots.

Aim for Heart-Level Impact: Good teaching isn't just about correct answers; it's about inspiring moral insight, compassion, and change.

Think of a moral or spiritual truth you want to convey—how might a story achieve what a lecture cannot?

What daily encounters could become parables, helping others see deeper truths?

How can you nurture reflection and imagination, so you're ready to teach in ways that engage both heart and mind?

Proverbs 1:6 | 2 Samuel 12:1–7

Day 6 — Luke 24:13-35

Remember Like Jesus

The Road to Remembering

Two disciples trudged along the road back home to Emmaus. They were tired and disheartened. Jesus had been crucified; now He was rumored to be alive, his followers walked the tension of confusion and disappointment. As they journeyed, a stranger joined them—Jesus Himself, though they didn't recognize Him. Instead of revealing His identity outright, Jesus did something profound: He helped them remember. He began with Scripture, recounting God's faithful dealings with Israel, showing them that their present sorrow fit into a larger redemptive story. Through these memories, He transformed their disillusionment into understanding.

When they stopped to eat, Jesus broke bread. In that ordinary yet meaningful action—a simple meal echoing the Last Supper—the disciples recognized Him. The memory of what Jesus had done and taught sparked new clarity. This was no nostalgic look backward; it propelled them forward, reorienting their perspective in the light of God's ongoing work.

Remembering with Purpose

Jesus shows us that remembering isn't about clinging to the past as a comfort blanket. Rather, it's a dynamic act that connects history with hope. On the Emmaus road, He recalled events and He reframed them. By anchoring the disciples in God's faithfulness throughout the ages and then tying that history to the risen Christ before them, He revealed that remembrance can shatter despair and rekindle expectancy.

When Jesus instituted the Lord's Supper He used ordinary elements to trigger sacred memory. Bread and wine became symbols that, when remembered properly, open our eyes to God's love and purpose. Similarly, our own remembrance isn't passive longing for "the good old days" but an invitation to see how God's steady hand guides both past and present, shaping our future with promise.

How Now?

Reflect on God's Story: Like Jesus, let Scripture guide you. Identify patterns of God's faithfulness in biblical history and in your own life story.

Reframe Your Present: When discouragement hits, recall how God has delivered, provided, and restored before. Let these memories shift your current perspective toward hope.

Use Tangible Reminders: Simple acts—sharing a meal, lighting a candle, journaling answered prayers—can serve as touchpoints that awaken gratitude and awareness.

Tell the Stories: Speak openly about how God has acted in your life and in the lives of others. Storytelling cements memory, encourages faith, and opens spiritual eyes.

When you feel stuck or disillusioned, how can remembering God's past faithfulness reshape your current outlook?

What simple, everyday practices or symbols can you use to keep God's works fresh in your mind?

In what ways can you share stories of God's faithfulness with others, helping them remember and find renewed hope?

Luke 22:19-20 | Psalm 105:5 | Joshua 4:4-7

Day 7 — Mark 1:35

Retreat Like Jesus

Finding Stillness

Before dawn, while the towns were still quiet and most people were asleep, Jesus slipped away. He stepped out of the city's crowded streets and headed toward the outskirts—desolate places where the hum of voices and the press of needs faded. There, surrounded by silence, Jesus listened and prayed. He didn't do this once or twice, but often. Jesus regularly withdrew to quiet spaces. In the stillness, Jesus could still His mind- He could search his heart as he sought after His Father's.

Retreat wasn't an escape born of fear or simple weariness. It was a deliberate rhythm. With so many seeking His teaching and healing, one might expect Jesus to maximize every moment with more doing. Instead, He chose to rise early, move beyond the reach of expectation, and find renewal in solitude.

A New Pace

Jesus knew true strength doesn't come from running faster or doing more. It springs from a deeper well than human effort can reach. By retreating into quiet places, He acknowledged human limits and modeled a pace that refused to let urgency define every decision. In the wilderness—often a symbol of testing and scarcity—Jesus found clarity and purpose. Rest isn't just a reward for hard work, the end of effort; it's the beginning of effort, the foundational practice shaping how we engage the world.

We often avoid quiet reflection, afraid of what we might discover within ourselves. Yet these honest moments before God bring healing and authenticity. Retreat also serves as a launch point rather than an endpoint. Emerging from solitude, we carry renewed purpose into our responsibilities—more attuned to God's presence, better equipped to serve, love, and create in alignment with His desires.

How Now?

Create a Rhythm of Retreat: Identify a place or time in your routine to be alone—away from screens, conversations, and clamor.

Embrace the Wilderness: Don't fear moments of silence or emptiness. Let them be sacred opportunities to listen, reflect, and reconnect with God's voice.

Trust the Slow Work: Resist the urge to measure worth by busyness. See rest as an act of faith, trusting that God can work through you more fully when you're centered in Him.

Where can you carve out a "desolate place" in your life—physically or mentally—to pause and pray?

What fears keep you from stepping away for solitude and silence?

How might regular, quiet retreat bring renewed clarity and purpose to your daily demands?

Luke 5:16 | Psalm 46:10 | 1 Kings 19:11–13

Day 8   Mark 14:60-61

Silent Like Jesus

When Stillness Speaks Louder Than Words

Jesus stood while false accusations and twisted truths swirled around Him. Religious leaders, political powers, and His very own people, waited for His defense. Instead, He chose silence. As the unjust trial that led to His death unfolded, Jesus remained silent. This wasn't resignation or weakness; it was a deliberate, faith-filled decision. As Isaiah foretold of the suffering servant who would remain quiet under oppression, Jesus held His ground calmly. His silence spoke volumes—rooted not in clever arguments, but in trust that God's justice would prevail.

Beyond the dramatic moments leading to the cross, Jesus also exercised silence in everyday confrontations. When cornered by religious leaders eager to trap Him, He sometimes responded with a question or no response at all. He knew that endless debate rarely changes hearts. By choosing when to speak and when to remain silent, He allowed truth to shine on its own, undimmed by fruitless disputes.

Quiet Strength and Unshaken Trust

We often feel compelled to respond immediately when misunderstood or provoked, fearing silence might signal weakness. Yet Jesus shows that sometimes quiet restraint is the most faithful response. By holding back our words, we release the need to control perceptions and outcomes, placing our confidence in God as our primary authority.

Silence can disarm hostility, allowing space for the Holy Spirit to work in ways our words cannot. It acknowledges that not every claim requires a rebuttal, not every confrontation a comeback. Jesus' silence wasn't passive—it was active trust. His example challenges us to weigh our words carefully and recognize that some truths shine brighter without our constant commentary.

How Now?

Pause Before Speaking: Next time someone's words sting, take a breath. Ask if speaking now will truly bring peace or clarity, or if silence might serve better.

Let Actions Speak: Integrity, kindness, and faithfulness can communicate more profoundly than any rebuttal.

Trust God's Timing: Silence can demonstrate faith that God, who sees all, will handle what lies beyond our control.

In what situations do you feel most tempted to argue unnecessarily?

How can embracing silence show trust in God's truth and justice?

When might silence open a door for the Holy Spirit to work where your words can't?

Isaiah 53:7 | Proverbs 26:4 | Ecclesiastes 3:7

Day 9   Matthew 16:13-28

Talk Like Jesus

Truth Without Tearing Down

Jesus and the disciples neared a town believed by many to be the gateway to the underworld. Here, He turned to His disciples and asked a question that still carries the weight of belief and faith: "Who do you say that I am?" It was Peter—one of Jesus' closest followers—who confidently proclaimed, "You are the Christ, the Son of the living God."

In this place, known as the entrance (or exit) of Hades, Peter declared that Jesus was the One who would rescue the world from sin and death. Jesus commended Peter for his insight, recognizing that such wisdom came from the Father. Peter got it—or so it seemed.

Not long after, Jesus spoke of His impending suffering and execution. Peter was quick to object. He couldn't fathom what Jesus described—Jesus was far too important and powerful to suffer! With urgency, Peter rejected the idea outright.

Jesus responded with words that might seem harsh to our ears: "Get behind me, Satan!" Yet, His rebuke was not an attack—it was a loving correction. He wasn't just confronting Peter's misunderstanding; He was waking him up to the twisted schemes of the enemy. Jesus redirected Peter, reorienting him toward the ways of the kingdom.

Notice what Jesus *didn't* do. He didn't bring up Peter's mistake again. He didn't recount it to the other disciples. If there was anyone Jesus could have made an example of, it was Peter. But Jesus addressed the issue directly—and then moved on.

Words That Build, Not Break

Talking like Jesus means choosing words that heal, especially when someone frustrates or disappoints us. Jesus corrected missteps directly and privately, preserving relationships and honoring the dignity of those involved. No vilifying, no slander, no belittling or scandalizing—just honest, loving correction.

When we're hurt or offended, it's easy to gossip or vent in search of validation from others. But Jesus shows us a better way: to address wrongdoing face-to-face with both grace and truth. This approach fosters connection over division and ensures that our words reflect the worth of others, even in their failures.

How Now?

Confront Privately and Kindly: If someone wrongs you, speak to them directly, respectfully, and lovingly.

Avoid Gossip: Before sharing someone's failings, ask yourself if it's necessary or helpful. Will it build them up or tear them down?

Honor Their Dignity: Remember that every person bears God's image. Speak in ways that respect their worth, even when addressing a mistake.

Think of a recent conflict—how did you speak about the other person afterward? Would it align with how Jesus handled similar tensions?

What steps can you take to resist the urge to gossip or rant when someone disappoints you?

How might talking like Jesus reshape your relationships and create an environment of trust and growth?

Leviticus 19:16 | Ephesians 4:29 | Proverbs 15:1

Day 10   Personal Reflection

Mark 3:20-34

The house was packed. Jesus had barely stepped inside before a crowd formed, spilling into the yard. People pushed and craned their necks, hoping to catch a glimpse of Him. So much was happening that there wasn't even time to eat. His family, hearing of all that was happening, showed up to bring Him home. Whatever was happening, it was getting too big, drawing too much attention, and creating the start of what could be a dangerous movement. "He's out of His mind," they said, convinced He'd gone too far.

The religious leaders from Jerusalem got wind of all the excitement and fanfare. They made their own accusations to squelch the excitement building around Jesus: "He's possessed by Satan. That's how He drives out demons—with the devil's power."

Jesus called them over, calm but direct. He spoke in stories, knowing how powerful a good metaphor can be. "How can Satan drive out Satan? A kingdom divided against itself is doomed. A family at war with itself will collapse. If I'm using the devil's power, then wouldn't that mean his kingdom is self-destructing? That doesn't even make sense.

"Let me put it another way: You can't rob a strong man's house without tying him up first. Only then can you take what's his. What I'm doing is binding the strong man—Satan—and reclaiming what doesn't belong to him.

"Listen carefully: Every sin, every mistake, every word spoken out of line can be forgiven. But if you refuse to see the Spirit's work for what it is—if you reject God's presence right in front of you—that's a sin you'll carry with you forever."

He was blunt because the religious leaders had accused Him of working for the devil when it was clearly God moving through Him.

Meanwhile, His family was still outside, trying to get to Him. Someone whispered to Jesus, "Your mother and brothers are here. They're asking for You."

Jesus looked around the room, at the people sitting near Him, hanging on His every word. "Who is My mother? Who are My brothers?" He asked, not to dismiss His family but to broaden the idea of connection. He gestured to the crowd. "Here. This is My family. Whoever aligns themselves with God's purpose—that's My brother, sister, and mother."

What about this encounter relates to your own life? What aspects of who Jesus connects to what it means to be human?

What actions does this story inspire you to take?

Day 11 — Luke 8:1–3

Impartial Like Jesus

Hearts, Not Hierarchies

As Jesus traveled from one town to another, proclaiming the good news of God's kingdom, a small band of followers accompanied Him. Among them were several women who supported His ministry with their own resources. One was Joanna, the wife of Chuza, a manager in Herod's household. Joanna was connected to wealth and power—someone who could have opened doors, wielded influence, and legitimized Jesus' mission in the eyes of the elite.

Yet Jesus never sought to leverage Joanna's status to gain political traction or financial security. He didn't alter His message to appeal to the powerful, nor did He depend on the wealthy to endorse His ministry. Jesus' mission wasn't driven by donations, networks, or the favor of influential patrons. Instead, He remained impartial, treating every person—rich or poor, famous or forgotten—with equal dignity and importance.

Kingdom Over Connections

Our world often assumes that connecting with the right people or amassing enough resources ensures success. It's tempting to believe that wealth and influence are necessary tools for advancing even spiritual endeavors. But Jesus challenges this mindset.

Jesus had well-connected followers, yet He never depended on their status to spread His message. He valued hearts over hierarchies, focusing on people rather than positions. His impartiality shows that God's kingdom doesn't advance through political endorsements or financial might. Instead, it grows through faithful obedience, sacrificial love, and the Spirit's work in ordinary lives.

This isn't a condemnation of wealth or influence—it's a reminder that they're not the foundation of God's work. The smallest acts of service, the quietest prayers, and the humblest believers all have vital roles in His unfolding story. Jesus teaches us that true impact comes not from courting power, but from trusting God's methods and remaining faithful wherever we are.

How Now?

Check Your Motives: When forming partnerships or building relationships, ask if you're seeking kingdom purposes or personal advantages.

See Each Person's Worth: Don't be swayed by wealth, status, or reputation. Treat all people as beloved children of God, worthy of respect and attention.

Trust God's Pathways: Instead of trying to influence the world by worldly means, trust that God's Spirit works through humility, truth, and faithful endurance.

How have you been tempted to rely on someone's wealth or connections to achieve a "kingdom" goal?

In what ways can you affirm the dignity of those society overlooks or undervalues?

How can you shift your perspective to value faithfulness over influence, trusting that God's power isn't limited by human resources?

James 2:1–4 | 1 Corinthians 1:26–29 | 2 Kings 7:3–9

Day 12   Mark 1:14–15

Witness Like Jesus

Simple Words, Tangible Actions

In the early days of His ministry, Jesus entered towns and villages with a simple proclamation: *"Good news—the kingdom of God is near."* It was a familiar phrase in the Roman world. Heralds would announce "good news" whenever an emperor made a decree or introduced a new law. These announcements often came with increased taxes, new restrictions, or shifting political landscapes.

Jesus' announcement was different. His *good news* wasn't tied to demands from earthly rulers. It carried the promise of God's restoring presence. With compassion and authority, Jesus invited people to recognize that God's reality was breaking into theirs.

As He moved through these spaces, Jesus embodied the kingdom He proclaimed. He healed the sick, uplifted the poor, and forgave the sinner, demonstrating that His message was more than words—it was a tangible reality. His witness wasn't complicated or wrapped in complex theology. It was simple, direct, and alive in His actions.

Living the Truth

Witnessing is often viewed as reciting memorized lines or having the perfect theological response. But Jesus shows us that witnessing is as simple as living out the truth we've encountered.

Jesus began with just a few words—*"Good news, the kingdom is near"*—and let His life fill in the details. In the same way, we don't need to force conversations or present long-winded explanations. People are drawn to authenticity. If Jesus is the reality we're pursuing, He will be the reality others see—and they will be drawn to Him.

When people notice our hope, peace, or compassionate responses, they may wonder what fuels this difference. The answer is Jesus. Witnessing like Him isn't about having all the right words in a perfect script. It's about allowing the kingdom's reality to flow through our actions and words, inviting others to see God's presence in us.

How Now?

Embody the Message: Focus on living in a way that reflects Christ's love, patience, and generosity, rather than perfect explanations.

Speak Simply: When asked about your faith, start with what matters most—the goodness of God's love and the hope Jesus brings.

Trust Authentic Relationships: Share your faith naturally within the context of honest relationships. Let curiosity and friendship open doors for deeper conversations.

Demonstrate Consistency: Words alone can't carry the message. Show consistency between what you say and how you live, allowing integrity to deepen your witness.

How can you simplify the way you share your faith, focusing on what truly matters?

What are some small yet tangible ways you can embody God's kingdom in your daily life?

Who in your life might be drawn closer to God by seeing His reality reflected through your actions and attitude?

Colossians 4:5-6 | Proverbs 11:30 | 1 Peter 3:15

Day 13   Luke 7:36–50

Comfortable Like Jesus

Grace in the Awkward Moments

Jesus reclined at a table in the home of a Pharisee named Simon. The room buzzed with social norms that slowly shifted to whispered judgments. A "sinful" woman had stepped into the scene and knelt beside Jesus. Without a word, she began to wash His feet with her tears, dry them with her hair, and anoint them with costly perfume.

This wasn't just a break in etiquette; it was downright awkward. The silence grew heavy as everyone struggled to make sense of her actions. The guests likely felt uncomfortable and perplexed, unsure how to respond.

Jesus, however, was comfortable with discomfort. He recognized her act of profound devotion and repentance. Instead of pushing away the awkwardness or dismissing the woman as inappropriate, Jesus embraced the moment. He commended her, reframed her actions as a "beautiful thing," and exposed the shallowness of those who refused to see beyond appearances. Jesus turned an unsettling scene into an opportunity for grace and revelation.

The Gift of Awkwardness

How often do we flee from uncomfortable moments—silence in a conversation, a person who doesn't fit socially, or someone holding an opinion that unsettles us? We tend to stick with what's comfortable, associating with those who mirror our values, communicate smoothly, or make us feel at ease.

Jesus models a different approach. He stepped toward the discomfort, even when it broke cultural norms. He honored the humanity and heart of the person at the center of the tension.

This challenges us to rethink how we handle awkwardness. Instead of seeing discomfort as a sign something's wrong, what if we viewed it as a doorway to deeper understanding and compassion? Actions that feel socially jarring may carry profound spiritual significance. Those who behave differently, struggle to communicate, or bring tension into our conversations may hold truths we need to hear. Jesus' willingness to embrace awkwardness invites us to slow down, look deeper, and ask: "Do I see this person the way God does?" Rather than dismissing, ignoring, or mocking what feels strange, we can choose to listen, learn, and love.

How Now?

Lean Into Discomfort: When conversations stall or someone's mannerisms feel strange, stay present and attentive.

See Beyond Labels: Don't let stigmas and cultural bias prevent you from recognizing the God-given worth in others.

Practice Hospitality in Awkwardness: Welcome those who struggle to fit in. Offer a listening ear, a smile, or a simple act of kindness, trusting that God can work through even the most uncomfortable exchanges.

What makes you feel most uncomfortable in social settings, and why?

How might embracing rather than avoiding awkward moments help you grow in compassion and understanding?

In what ways can you make room in your life for people who don't fit neatly into your social comfort zone?

Mark 2:16-17 | Romans 12:10 | John 4:4-26

Day 14   Matthew 3:13–17

Obey Like Jesus

Faithfulness in the Small Things

Huge crowds had gathered at the Jordan River to see John the Baptist, to repent, and to be baptized, seeking a new start. Then Jesus stepped into the water, ready to be baptized Himself. Onlookers were confused. John was confused and resisted at first—why would the sinless One need this sign of repentance? Those watching might have wondered the same. It seemed unnecessary, even puzzling.

But Jesus insisted. Though He had no sins to confess, He embraced this humble act of obedience as part of God's unfolding plan. By entering those waters, Jesus aligned Himself with humanity's journey toward God and set a pattern for His entire ministry. His baptism wasn't a grand miracle or a crisis moment—it was a simple yet profound step of faithfulness. If He was willing to obey in something that appeared so unnecessary, how much more would He trust the Father's will when facing greater challenges?

Obedience as a Lifestyle

We often think of obedience as reserved for life's big decisions—career moves, moral crossroads, or defining sacrifices. But Jesus shows us that faithfulness begins in moments that may seem unnecessary or overly simple. His baptism, while perplexing to onlookers, was an act of honoring God's direction. Such obedience trained His heart to choose God's way over personal logic, comfort, or reputation.

For us, obeying in these seemingly trivial matters—offering kindness when it's inconvenient, speaking truth when it's awkward, stepping forward when we'd rather hold back, shapes who we become. It builds spiritual resilience and prepares us for greater tests of faith. Over time, these simple acts of surrender accumulate into a lifestyle that, like Jesus', can stand firm even when the path leads through trials and challenges.

How Now?

Start Where You Are: Identify a small act of obedience God might be nudging you to take. Follow through, even if it feels unnecessary or confusing at the moment.

Trust God's Bigger Picture: Like Jesus at His baptism, recognize that obedience may have meaning beyond your current perspective. Over time, you'll see how these steps fit into God's larger plan.

Build Faithfulness Gradually: Each act of obedience strengthens your capacity to trust God. Allow these moments to train your heart for greater acts of faith down the road.

Embrace Humility: Obedience often involves setting aside pride. Whether it's a ritual like baptism or a mundane gesture of service, consider what it means to lower yourself in love and surrender.

What step of obedience feels unnecessary or puzzling to you right now?

How might embracing that step prepare you for more significant challenges in the future?

In what ways can you cultivate a heart that readily aligns with God's will, even when it doesn't make immediate sense?

John 14:15 | Philippians 2:5-8 | 1 Samuel 15:22

Day 15   Luke 10:17-20

Celebrate Like Jesus

Joy That Lasts

The disciples returned from their mission beaming with excitement. They had gone out as Jesus instructed—preaching the kingdom, healing the sick, and even casting out demons. Things had gone better than they dared hope. Extraordinary signs unfolded at their touch, enemies retreated, and broken lives found restoration. Enthusiastically, they rushed to tell Jesus everything, their excitement spilling into every word: *"Lord, even the demons submit to us in Your name!"*

But Jesus responded in a surprising way. Instead of cheering their successes or fueling their pride, He redirected their celebration. While acknowledging the power they had wielded, He urged them: *"Do not rejoice that the spirits submit to you, but rejoice that your names are written in heaven."*

In other words, Jesus invited them to celebrate what truly matters—the unshakable reality of their belonging in God's family, not the fleeting thrill of ministry achievements.

Rooted in Lasting Joy

We often tie our celebrations to accomplishments, milestones, and outward signs of success. The disciples did the same, focusing on what they had done rather than who they were in Christ. Jesus lovingly nudged them toward a deeper joy—one that isn't rooted in spectacular moments or extraordinary results, but in their eternal connection to God.

In our lives, it's easy to revel in promotions, victories, or recognition. While it's not wrong to acknowledge successes, Jesus reminds us to ground our greatest joy in what endures. Achievements come and go, but what's permanent—and worth celebrating—is our relationship with God, the grace that secures our place in His kingdom, and the hope of eternal life.

This perspective doesn't diminish the good that's done or the healing we see. Instead, it ensures that those manifestations of God's power point us back to Him, not ourselves. When we celebrate the Giver rather than just the gifts, we keep our hearts aligned with God's purposes. This eternal perspective keeps us humble, grateful, and focused on what is truly worth celebrating.

How Now?

Celebrate the Eternal: Shift your focus from temporary accomplishments to the eternal truth of being God's beloved child.

Acknowledge Achievements, Keep Perspective: Be grateful for success or progress, remember that these are secondary to your relationship with God.

Find Joy in Identity: Your worth doesn't hinge on how much you do or how well you perform. Rejoice in the unchanging reality that you are known and loved by God.

What do you typically celebrate in your life? How might you focus more on the eternal rather than the temporary?

How can recognizing that your name is "written in heaven" shape your response to both triumphs and setbacks?

In what ways can you regularly practice celebrating God's faithfulness and your identity in Him instead of merely external accomplishments?

Matthew 6:33 | Philippians 3:20 | Psalm 126:3

Day 16 — Luke 2:52

Work Like Jesus

Hands That Build

What would Jesus' hands feel like if you had the chance to shake them? Not the scarred hands Thomas touched, before that—even before He was known as a teacher, before anyone whispered His name as Savior. Imagine Jesus' hands rough and calloused, hands that held tools to smooth wood and cut stone, hands that bore the marks of labor.

We often picture Jesus teaching multitudes, healing the sick, or calming storms. But for much of His life, He worked as a tradesman, a builder and carpenter. Jesus spent years learning and mastering His trade.

For over half of His life, Jesus worked among peers, friends, and neighbors. He contributed to His community, bringing stability to His family, earning respect as someone who grew "in favor with God and man." This often-overlooked season of His life shaped Him. Before His public ministry, before the miracles and parables, the confrontations and controversies, He was faithful in the daily, physical, and sometimes mundane work of a tradesman.

The Sacredness of Work

Work can often feel like a means to an end—a way to survive, climb the ladder, or escape into retirement. Work wasn't a burden for Jesus, it was an opportunity to serve, grow in patience and skill, and honor God.

Carpentry likely wasn't what Jesus chose, it was the family trade, woven into His life's fabric. In it, He worked with excellence, using His trade to bless others and glorify God.

What if, instead of viewing work as a frustrating "have to," we saw it as a meaningful "get to"? A chance to grow in humility, diligence, and purpose. Paul reminds us in *Colossians 3:23*: *"Whatever you do, work at it with all your heart, as working for the Lord, not for human masters."* This perspective transforms our work—whether we're building furniture, balancing spreadsheets, or teaching students. When we see our labor as a reflection of our faith, it has the potential to move us from a daily grind to an act of worship.

How Now?

Reframe Your Workday: Start your day by dedicating your work to God. Pause before tasks to remember that each effort, no matter how small, has the potential to glorify Him.

Excel in Your Craft: Whether you're writing, building, or teaching, approach your tasks with the mindset of a craftsman—seeking excellence in every detail.

Find Meaning in the Mundane: Jesus likely worked on repetitive or unimpressive projects. Yet He brought dignity to the ordinary. Consider how you might approach mundane tasks with fresh purpose.

What does it mean for you to humbly pursue your work as if it's a craft?

How can you reshape your attitude toward work to make it an act of worship?

What small changes could you make in your daily work to reflect excellence and serve others?

Colossians 3:23 | Ecclesiastes 9:10 | Proverbs 22:29

Day 17   Luke 7:43

Eat Like Jesus

A Table of Grace

Jesus spent so much time around the table—enjoying food, savoring conversation, and welcoming companions—that His opponents tried to use it against Him. The narrative about Jesus shows Him dining with His disciples, their families, longtime friends, and even strangers He met along the road. He attended gatherings and feasts, sitting with people from all walks of life—especially those pushed to the margins of society.

Religious leaders accused Him of being a glutton and a drunkard. Overindulgence wasn't the real problem—it was that Jesus willingly shared His meals with those on the edges of society. For Jesus, the table wasn't just a place to eat; it was a place to connect, to show acceptance, and to extend grace.

In a culture where hospitality was central, sharing a meal meant accepting someone and welcoming them into your life. Most people gladly offered hospitality to those like them—the same tribe, political group, or religion. Venturing beyond boundaries was uncommon, even scandalous. Jesus wasn't like most people. He used the table to demonstrate the radical inclusivity of God's kingdom, gathering tax collectors, fishermen, the poor, and the sick. Jesus extended acceptance where it was least expected.

These meals often became moments of transformation. Those once pushed aside found their place in God's unfolding story.

Hospitality as Sacred Work

Our gatherings may look different now—around a dining room table, a restaurant booth, or even a breakroom. Yet the simple act of sharing food and conversation still holds power. Who we invite, how we welcome them, and the intentionality we bring to our time together can reflect the love and grace Jesus demonstrated. When we invite others to a meal, we say, *"You matter to me."* When we extend that invitation to those who feel marginalized or overlooked, we mirror Jesus' example of hospitality.

For Jesus, mealtime wasn't just about physical nourishment; it provided relational nourishment, lifting the ordinary act of eating into a sacred space where hearts could be touched and lives changed. It is far too easy to lose touch even with those closest to us. Hospitality means treating strangers as if they have always belonged. What might happen if we approached meals with the hope of rebuilding connections, extending grace, and reflecting God's welcoming heart?

How Now?

Practice Intentional Hospitality: Invite someone new or someone who might feel excluded to share a meal.

Foster Genuine Conversation: Put away distractions. Ask meaningful questions, listen closely, and show sincere interest in the other person's story.

Reflect Kingdom Values: Remember that your hospitality, no matter how simple the meal, can communicate God's love, acceptance, and grace.

Where might you approach a meal with more intentionality, seeing it as a sacred time to connect and build others up?

Is there anyone God is prompting you to invite to your table?

Matthew 9:10 | Hebrews 10:24–25 | Romans 12:13

Day 18   Matthew 8:23–27

Sleep Like Jesus

Rest in Trust

In a world that glorifies endless productivity and non-stop activity, Jesus' choice to sleep in the middle of a storm is perhaps as wise as it is shocking. His rest was not reckless or negligent, His heart and mind were at peace. A non-anxious spirit can sleep soundly, trusting that even when we close our eyes God's care does not waver.

On that day in the boat, as the wind howled and waves lashed the hull, Jesus curled up and slept. It's not hard to imagine His disciples' disbelief as they struggled against the storm. They wondered to each other, *"How can He sleep at a time like this…doesn't He know we are in danger?"* Anxiety and urgency crashed like waves in their minds. When they did wake Jesus up… His calm response revealed His deep security in the Father's hands. With a gesture and a few words the chaos waters waned.

Jesus' nap was more than a footnote; it was a living illustration that rest is not wasted time, but a faithful practice of trust. By sleeping, Jesus acknowledged His human limits and God's infinite provision.

Why We Struggle to Rest

For many of us, cat naps and deep sleep feel like luxuries we can't afford. We lie awake, burdened by to-do lists or fears that if we stop, we'll lose ground. It's easy to equate busyness with worthiness. When we do it typically leaves us feeling restless and exhausted.

Jesus shows us that when little more can be done—when progress stalls and human effort hits a wall— it's a good time to release control. Sleep is an act of faith, a recognition that God continues His work even when we can't see it. Naps and lights out can indeed be holy acts of worship. As we drift into sleep, we can whisper a prayer, offering our efforts to God and asking Him to bless what we've done, knowing He will carry us and our concerns.

How Now?

Embrace Your Limits: Recognize that you are not infinite. Setting boundaries on work and worry can open space for genuine rest.

Make Rest a Prayerful Practice: As you lie down, pray that God would grant you peace of heart and mind. Release your unfinished tasks into His care.

Resist the Productivity Trap: Remember that your value is not measured by your output. Rest honors God by trusting Him more than your own relentless striving.

Seek Rhythms of Renewal: Just as Jesus slept to restore His strength, find regular pauses—quiet moments, short breaks, or full nights of rest—to renew your soul.

Where do you struggle to prioritize rest in your life, and what's driving that struggle?

How can you follow Jesus' example of peace and trust, even when life feels chaotic?

What is one tangible step you can take this week to view rest not as weakness, but as a necessary rhythm of faith?

Psalm 127:2 | Mark 6:31 | 1 Kings 19:5–7

Day 19   John 2:1–11

Wait Like Jesus

The Patience of Perfect Timing

Weddings in Jesus' time weren't single-day events; they stretched over days, sometimes weeks. These feasts were filled with laughter, music, and abundant celebration. At one such wedding in Cana, the celebration was in full swing when Mary, Jesus' mother, noticed a growing crisis: the wine had run out. No wine meant no more celebration—an embarrassment that could overshadow the couple's joyful beginning. Concerned for the hosts, Mary turned to Jesus.

Jesus was enjoying the festivities and conversation. Up until this point, He had lived quietly as a carpenter's son, patiently waiting for the right time to begin His public ministry. When Mary asked for His help, He responded, *"My time has not yet come."* —Jesus felt no prompting to reveal Himself through signs and wonders. Yet, Mary persisted, instructing the servants to follow His lead.

In this subtle encounter divine timing shifted. Jesus instructed the servants to fill large jars with water, and when they drew it out, it was wine—the finest the host had ever tasted. This was His first miracle, a small yet significant unveiling of who He truly was. For decades, Jesus had waited, preparing His heart and mind, faithfully working in ordinary life. Then, at just the right moment, He stepped into His role as Rescuer.

Active, Trusting Patience

Waiting like Jesus means trusting that God's plan unfolds in His perfect timing. For most of His adult life, Jesus toiled in obscurity, building tables and benches rather than reputations. He didn't rush to prove Himself or grow impatient for a stage. His waiting was active—shaped by prayer, obedience, and a heart fully tuned to the Spirit's guidance.

The dreams, callings, and desires that stir within us can carry immense weight. We may long to see them realized immediately, straining against delays or disappointments. But Jesus shows us that waiting is not wasted. God uses in-between moments to refine our character, align our desires, and prepare us for the work He has designed. To wait like Jesus is to trust that every season has purpose. When the time is right, God will release us into the purposes he has in store for us.

How Now?

Embrace the In-Between: View delays as seasons of preparation rather than setbacks. While waiting, cultivate a listening heart.

Resist the Urge to Hurry: Avoid forcing outcomes. Let your efforts be guided by patience and trust rather than impatience or fear.

Find Purpose in the Present: Invest in the people, tasks, and responsibilities you have right now, trusting that God is using them to shape you.

What vision or dream has God placed on your heart?

In what ways might you be rushing ahead, rather than allowing God to prepare you for the right moment?

How has God used past seasons of waiting to prepare you for something greater?

How can you more fully trust God's timing this week, especially in areas where waiting feels difficult?

James 5:7-8 | Psalm 37:7 | Isaiah 40:31

Day 20   Personal reflection day

Matthew 4:1-17

Then Jesus was led by the Spirit into the wilderness, a desolate and harsh place. He spent forty days and forty nights there, fasting and preparing for what was ahead. As the days passed, hunger gnawed at Him, making Him physically weak but spiritually focused.

That's when the tempter showed up. "If you're really the Son of God, turn these stones into bread," he said, a sly challenge aimed at exploiting Jesus' hunger pains.

Jesus didn't flinch. "Scripture says, 'People don't live on bread alone, but on every word that comes from God.'"

The devil didn't stop there. He took Jesus to Jerusalem, to the highest point of the temple. "If you're really the Son of God, jump off," he said, adding a twist of scripture: "After all, doesn't it say, 'God will command His angels to catch you so you won't even stub your toe?'"

Jesus stood firm. "It's also written: 'Don't test the Lord your God.'"

Finally, the devil took Jesus to a high mountain, showing Him all the kingdoms of the world and their wealth and splendor. "I'll give it all to You," he said, "if You bow down and worship me."

Jesus had heard enough. "Get out of here, Satan. Scripture says, 'Worship the Lord your God and serve Him only.'"

The devil left, and angels arrived, caring for Jesus as He regained His strength.

Not long after, Jesus returned to Galilee. John the Baptist had been arrested, and the news spread quickly. But Jesus stayed focused. He left Nazareth, His hometown, and moved to Capernaum, a town by the sea in the region of Zebulun and Naphtali. It was a strategic and symbolic move, fulfilling the words of the prophet Isaiah: "The people who walked in darkness have seen a great light; on those living in the shadow of death, a light has dawned."

In Capernaum, Jesus began to build His ministry. This wasn't just a place to live; it became the hub of His teaching, healing, and the movement He was starting. The region was diverse, a crossroads of cultures and ideas, and Jesus immersed Himself in the lives of the people there. He began teaching in earnest, saying, "Change your direction. God's kingdom is here. It's time to live differently."

What about this encounter relates to your own life? What aspects of who Jesus connects to what it means to be human?

What actions does this story inspire you to take?

Day 21 — John 2:13–17

Fight Like Jesus

Confronting Injustice with Purpose

The Passover festival drew crowds of pilgrims into the temple courts—a place for worship, prayer, and communion. What Jesus encountered wasn't reverence or devotion- it was the clatter of money changing hands, the shuffle of livestock penned for sale, and the sharp exchange of profits. The weak and the poor, who came longing to draw near to God, were confronted with barriers and exploitation.

Jesus surveyed the scene and took action. He fashioned a cord into a whip, driving out the livestock and overturning the tables of the money-changers. It was a startling sight—the one who welcomed children and dined with outcasts was now disrupting commerce in the temple. Coins rolled across the dusty ground, animals scattered into the streets, and the supposed "helpers" of the temple were exposed for their greed.

Jesus' actions weren't about harming individuals. His aim was to dismantle an unjust system that enriched the powerful while keeping ordinary people distant from genuine worship. His actions revealed the heart of the problem: greed and corruption masquerading as faithfulness.

Restoration, Not Destruction

Jesus didn't "fight" the way we often think of fighting. He didn't lash out indiscriminately or seek revenge. Instead, He confronted the structures and practices that warped faith and burdened the vulnerable. His protest was measured and purposeful, exposing greed and corruption while calling people back to the heart of worship.

How easy is it for us to confuse attacking others with standing up for what's right? How easy is it to fight to protect our comfort rather than freeing others from oppression? Fighting like Jesus involves recognizing that true enemies are not individuals but the social, economic, or religious systems that cause harm, exclude the marginalized, and hinder access to God's grace.

We are invited to take stands against injustice with the intention of healing and uplifting rather than humiliating. Fighting like Jesus is not about venting our anger or winning arguments; it's about bravely confronting what's broken so that others might experience freedom, justice, and unhindered access to God.

How Now?

Identify the Real Issue: Before you "fight," ask yourself what you're truly fighting against. Is it a person, or a system that needs reform? Focus on dismantling the structure of injustice rather than attacking individuals.

Act with Purpose, Not Rage: Jesus' response was controlled and meaningful, not chaotic or vindictive. Consider how you can protest wrongs thoughtfully, guided by love and truth.

Aim for Restoration: Our goal is not to crush opponents, but to restore right relationships—between people and God, and among each other.

Think of a situation you find troubling: how are you focused on defeating "enemies" or changing the conditions that harm people?

Where can you use your voice, influence, or resources to challenge systems that exclude or exploit others?

How can you ensure that your response to injustice remains guided by love and the desire for restoration, rather than anger or self-interest?

Micah 6:8 | Ephesians 6:12 | Proverbs 31:8-9

Day 22   John 5:1–9

Ask Like Jesus

Inviting Reflection Through Questions

Jesus asked a lot of questions—more than 300 recorded in the annals of His life and ministry. Sometimes He questioned to provoke thought, sometimes to challenge assumptions, and often to help people uncover what they truly believed or desired. Many of those questions had seemingly "self-evident" answers. But Jesus used questions for more than receiving a reply. His questions created space for discovery—inviting people to recognize their own needs and hopes.

Consider the man at the pool of Bethesda.. He had been waiting by those waters for decades, longing for healing that never came. Jesus approached without assuming, inquiring what the man wanted. Jesus' question seemed almost too simple: "Do you want to get well?" The question invoked awareness beyond the obvious—it was an invitation for the man to reflect on his desires and confront the barriers holding him back.

The Power of a Well-Placed Question

We rarely have the profound insight into others' motives that Jesus did. Still, we can learn from His approach. How often do we skip asking questions because we think we already know what someone needs? How often do we jump ahead with advice or assumptions, missing opportunities to hear alternative perspectives? Questions create space for reflection, helping others uncover untold stories, mixed motives, and hidden hopes.

Asking questions like Jesus isn't about interrogation or prying—it's about invitation. It's asking, "What do you truly desire?" or "How are you really feeling?" and then listening—fully and openly. This approach helps us avoid assumptions and fosters deeper empathy and understanding. By asking questions that open doors rather than close them, we honor the complexity and dignity of each person's journey.

How Now?

Keep It Simple: Ask questions that are clear and honest, without pretense or over-complication.

Be Present: Tailor your questions to the moment and the person in front of you, showing that you're fully engaged.

Focus on Awareness: Questions don't always need to produce answers; sometimes their purpose is to help others see themselves more clearly.

Stay Curious: Asking questions like "What are you looking for?" (John 1:38) signals open-mindedness and genuine interest in another's journey.

What would it look like for you to use questions to encourage growth and understanding in your relationships?

What might change in your relationships if you replaced advice with thoughtful, open-ended questions?

Matthew 16:13–20 | Mark 10:51 | Matthew 22:15–22

Day 23   Luke 19:41–42

Cry Like Jesus

Tears That Heal

Jesus stood on a small hill overlooking Jerusalem, tears welling in his eyes. Thousands of pilgrims filled the city with the noise, smells, and anticipation of the Passover festival. He could hear merchants haggling, smell fresh bread baking, and catch the distant melody of songs sung by travelers eager to celebrate deliverance from oppression.

Amidst all these signs of devotion, Jesus saw something else: hearts trapped in rituals that no longer awakened them to God's presence. Like sheep without a shepherd, His own people stumbled forward, lost in a cycle of missed opportunities and spiritual numbness. He longed to bring them closer, to embrace them like a parent gathering a child into their arms. Their resistance grieved Him deeply.

Just days earlier, He had wept at the tomb of His friend Lazarus—lamenting death's sting. Now He wept over a city wearing its own kind of grave clothes, unaware of how far it stood from the life He offered.

Tears as Prayers

We often imagine strength as stoicism, but Jesus shatters that assumption by weeping openly. His tears for Lazarus and Jerusalem weren't signs of weakness; they were expressions of profound empathy, love, and longing for restoration.

In the same way, we might look at those around us—our communities, cities, schools, workplaces—and see spiritual emptiness, lost hopes, or broken dreams. Rather than responding with judgment, what if we followed Jesus' example and allowed ourselves to grieve their disconnection and pain?

Tears can be prayers without words, acknowledging the brokenness we see and inviting us to share in God's longing for healing and wholeness. Crying like Jesus isn't about despair; it's about honest recognition of brokenness. When we weep over what's lost—be it a life, a city, or the souls of people we care about—we open ourselves to God's heart and invite healing into our shared story.

How Now?

Embrace Authentic Emotion: Give yourself permission to feel deeply. Tears aren't failures of faith; they're windows into your compassion.

Weep for Others: Consider those who are spiritually distant or hurting. Allow your sorrow to spark empathy, intercession, and loving engagement.

Slow Down and Feel: In a culture that rushes past pain, take time to sit with sadness—yours and others'. Let grief soften your heart rather than harden it.

Who in your life or community might need your empathetic tears instead of judgment or indifference?

How might embracing grief lead you to deeper compassion and a more Christ-like response?

In what ways can your tears become prayers, expressing your longing for restoration and wholeness in the world?

John 11:35 | Ecclesiastes 3:4 | Psalm 34:18

Day 24   Luke 24:13–32

Walk Like Jesus

Steps Guided by Purpose

Jesus moved with a unique intentionality during His life on earth. He was calm and unrushed, free from the frantic pace that often drives us. His steps were guided purpose—He wasn't pushed by others' expectations or hurried along by the pressures of the moment. Instead, Jesus walked in rhythm with the Father's guidance, listening deeply and responding as the Spirit led.

Once, Jesus decided to travel through Samaria—a route most Jews of His day avoided due to cultural and religious tensions. Rather than go around, He chose to go through. There He met a Samaritan woman at a water well, sparking a conversation that challenged social boundaries, restored dignity, and ultimately transformed a life. This encounter was the result of a journey defined by intentional, Spirit-led steps. Jesus' willingness to walk a path others shunned broke stereotypes and shattered barriers.

Walking with Intention

Unlike Jesus, we often choose the quickest, most familiar routes—physically and relationally. We hurry through our routines, ignoring nudges that might lead us off the beaten path. But Jesus shows us that walking with purpose can mean taking the unexpected way, trusting the Spirit's guidance rather than public opinion or personal comfort.

When we slow down and open ourselves to the possibility that God might have something significant for us beyond our usual paths—letting go of urgency, prejudice, and habit—we can discover encounters that transform us and bless others. Walking like Jesus is about more than just getting from point A to point B. It's about stepping into each moment with an openness to God's direction.

What if we carried that kind of mindfulness into our daily movements? Whether strolling down a hallway at work, driving through our neighborhood, or pushing a cart through the grocery store, each moment offers a chance to pay attention. It's not just about reaching a destination; it's about noticing where God might be nudging, who we might be called to see, and how we can participate in the redemptive work unfolding around us.

How Now?

Be Attentive to the Spirit's Nudges: Instead of rushing, pause to consider where God might be guiding you—even if it means adjusting your plans.

Embrace Unfamiliar Spaces: Don't shy away from people or places outside your comfort zone. Engaging beyond your usual boundaries can lead to unexpected growth.

Walk with Purpose, Not Pressure: Let go of urgency for urgency's sake. Move at a pace that leaves room for meaningful connection and divine appointments.

What areas of your life would benefit from slowing down and listening more closely to how the Spirit is leading?

Consider the paths you take each day—on foot, by car, or otherwise. What is Jesus inviting you to notice, change, or bring into those spaces?

How can you cultivate an openness to unexpected encounters that could lead to transformation—for you or someone else?

John 5:19 | Psalm 23:2-3 | Micah 6:8

Day 25   Luke 4:16

Worship Like Jesus

Habit, Not a Happenstance

The narratives about Jesus don't often contain the word "custom," so it's worth paying attention when it's used. And it is used to highlight Jesus's regular practice of attending the synagogue. This custom wasn't an incidental activity or a sporadic decision—it was intentional. Whether it was the particular synagogue in His hometown or simply His rhythm to engage with Scripture wherever He traveled, this practice of worship was woven into the pattern of His life.

For Jesus, worship wasn't just a private experience—it was communal. He joined others to hear God's Word, participate in discussions, and draw strength for His mission. His life blended prayer in solitude, acts of service, and shared meals with gatherings in worship. Jesus didn't compartmentalize His faith; instead, He lived out worship in a way that enriched His identity and aligned His actions with God's will.

Faith Flourishes in Community

In today's world, gatherings might look like Sunday services, fellowship groups, or informal meetings in homes. The principle remains unchanged: faith grows best in the fertile ground of community. Developing a custom of meeting with others isn't about rigid obligation but about creating a space for transformation.

Worshiping together keeps us steady when doubts creep in, distractions demand attention, or our energy wanes. It's a declaration that connecting with God and His people matters enough to prioritize, no matter how we feel.

Jesus didn't show up to log religious hours or fulfill a ritual. He engaged thoughtfully, honored tradition, and brought fresh insight and perspective. Beyond the walls of any building, His entire life became an expression of worship. From solitary prayer to compassionate action, Jesus showed us that what we learn in community shapes how we live in the world.

How Now?

Establish a Rhythm: Create a regular habit of gathering with others in worship. Whether formal or informal, let it be a consistent thread in your life.

Engage Fully: Show up with intention—listen, learn, and participate. Your presence and contributions can inspire and encourage others.

Live Worship Daily: Let what you experience in worship gatherings inspire your actions throughout the week. From serving others to seeking solitude in prayer, extend worship into your everyday life.

What would it look like for you to make worship a central habit in your life?

How can you bring fresh engagement to a gathering that feels routine or uninspiring?

In what ways can the truths you encounter in worship lead to concrete actions that reflect God's love?

Hebrews 10:24–25 | James 1:22 | Psalm 122:1 | Psalm 95:6–7

Day 26   Luke 6:12–16

Invest Like Jesus

Relational Depth That Transforms

The decision before Jesus was not one he took lightly. As he looked into the faces of the men who had been diligently following Him they returned a gaze of anticipation. They were intrigued by His message and inspired by His miracles and presence. They called Him—Rabbi—signifying their readiness to have their lives shaped by Him. As evening fell, He withdrew to a quiet hill slope, leaving behind the crowds and distractions. He spent the entire night in prayer, seeking His Father's wisdom for the critical choice before Him. When he returned to the group of ordinary people he chose from among them twelve who would receive a special kind of investment- a relational focus that was intentionally narrow and intense.

These twelve—fishermen, a tax collector, a zealot, and others—were a diverse and often conflicting mix of men who would have had little reason to remain together. Their willingness to follow and learn from Jesus bound them closer than any shared background could. Over three years, they would walk with Jesus, listen, observe, and learn from sunrise to sundown. This intentional investment shaped their character, clarified their calling, and equipped them to carry His message into the world.

Depth Over Breadth

While Jesus taught and served many, His most intentional investment was in a small group of people. Jesus demonstrates that true influence comes through personal, patient, and persistent relationship-building. Even in the narrow- Jesus didn't seek uniformity; He welcomed diversity, trusting that God could forge unity and purpose out of varied perspectives. This approach freed Him from the need to please the masses. By focusing on helping a few truly understand His ways, Jesus allowed truth to take root deeply before it spread broadly.

Quiet nights in prayer, patient teaching, and life-on-life mentoring reveal a strategy that values genuine transformation over quick recognition and flashy displays. Jesus demonstrated that lasting impact starts small and grows through faithful, focused investment.

How Now?

Choose Depth Over Breadth: Instead of trying to influence everyone at once, identify a small group of people—friends, family members, colleagues—whom you can walk alongside more closely.

Celebrate Diversity: Don't shy away from those who differ from you. Lean into diverse relationships as opportunities for growth and richer understanding.

Practice Patience: Transformation takes time. Be patient, persistent, and gracious, knowing that real growth rarely follows a straight line.

Who in your life could benefit from a more focused, intentional investment of your time and energy?

How can you embrace the differences in your closest relationships instead of avoiding or downplaying them?

How does Jesus' example challenge the way you prioritize relationships in your life?

Mark 3:13–19 | Proverbs 27:17 | 2 Timothy 2:2

Day 27   John 21:1–14

Cook Like Jesus

Meals That Heal

After His resurrection, Jesus met His disciples in unexpected ways, often meeting them right where they were. On one such occasion, He stood on a sandy beach by the Sea of Galilee in the early morning light. Kneeling over hot coals, He cooked fish and bread.

The disciples approached Him, carrying the weight of their past failures and fears—Peter, still stung by his denials, and the others, uncertain of their place after deserting Him. What they encountered wasn't a lecture or rebuke but the comforting aroma of a simple breakfast and an invitation: *"Come and have breakfast."*

In that moment, Jesus didn't just fill their empty stomachs; He bridged relational gaps. Over a meal anyone could have made—no special ingredients or advanced techniques—He restored trust and offered forgiveness. The simplicity of food became a pathway to reconciliation and renewal, reminding us that ordinary acts can carry extraordinary love.

Cooking as Connection

Today, meal preparation has become an outsourced task. With restaurants, caterers, and pre-packaged convenience, we often miss the personal touch that comes from preparing a meal ourselves. Jesus' example reminds us it's not about being a gourmet chef—His meal was as basic as it gets. Taking the time to cook for someone communicates far more than culinary skill; it says, *"You matter enough for me to invest my hands, my resources, and my time."*

In a world where pre-made options abound, choosing to cook becomes a heartfelt gesture of healing. Especially when tension or hurt exists in a relationship, preparing and sharing a meal offers an opportunity to extend grace. If you can make a sandwich, grill a burger or boil some noodles and sauce you can engage in this simple and powerful practice modeled by Jesus.

When others hurt or disappoint us the temptation is to wait for them to initiate- to apologize, or to reach out. Jesus shows us a different way. He took the initiative, extending grace by laying out bread and fish and inviting His disciples to eat. A meal prepared and offered in love has the power to soften hearts, restore connection, and re-establish community. This is the way of Jesus: the wounded healer who, instead of demanding apologies, sets a table of belonging and extends the first hand of reconciliation.

How Now?

Keep It Simple: Don't stress about an elaborate menu. A basic, thoughtfully prepared meal can speak volumes about your care and intentions.

Bridge the Gap: Consider someone with whom you have tension. Could a shared meal be a step toward understanding and forgiveness?

Take the Initiative: Don't wait for others to act. Be the one who sets the table and invites them in, just as Jesus did on the shoreline.

Who in your life could benefit from the simple gift of a home-cooked (home-prepared) meal right now—especially if there's been distance or hurt?

How might preparing even a basic dish help communicate care, respect, and a willingness to mend what's broken?

What holds you back from extending this kind of hospitality, and how might following Jesus' example free you to take the first step?

Romans 12:13 | Hebrews 13:2 | Proverbs 15:17

Day 28   Luke 5:17-26

See Like Jesus

Perceiving Hearts with Empathy and Discernment

In the crowded spaces of His ministry, Jesus often knew what others were thinking before they spoke a word. Was it divine insight? Or was His ability to perceive grounded in something deeper—His connection to the Father and His attentive awareness of human nature?

Jesus had a profound capacity to see beneath the surface. He discerned bitterness, fear, pride, curiosity, and longing in those around Him. This wasn't a mystical power reserved for the divine—it came from paying close attention and being deeply attuned to people's hearts.

When Jesus healed the paralytic and told him his sins were forgiven, the religious leaders *silently* questioned His authority. Jesus addressed their skepticism directly, not to humiliate or overpower them, but to invite them to confront their own hearts and consider who He truly was. Whether through compassion or correction, Jesus' goal was always restoration—guiding people toward the freedom and wholeness of God's kingdom.

Looking Deeper Through God's Lens

To see like Jesus isn't about reading minds or mastering the art of deduction. It's about cultivating a heart that seeks to understand and care for others. We begin with empathy, being fully present with people and recognizing the layers of hurt, hope, and humanity behind their actions.

Spiritual discernment is grounded in love, not suspicion. And discernment comes with responsibility. It's easy to misjudge or project our biases onto others, mistaking assumptions for truth. Jesus' example reminds us that seeing deeper should always serve the kingdom—it's about healing, understanding, and bringing light into dark places.

When we stay connected to God, we can look beyond surface behaviors and discern how to respond with grace and truth. Seeing like Jesus means looking at others through God's eyes, with a heart focused on restoration and love.

How Now?

Start with Empathy: Engage with others by listening deeply and seeking to understand their experiences, even when their actions frustrate or confuse you.

Pray for Discernment: Ask God to open your eyes to what's really happening in someone's heart and to guide your response.

Guard Against Misjudgment: Check your assumptions. Are you projecting your own fears or biases onto others? Let the Spirit lead, not your insecurities.

Focus on Restoration: Approach every interaction with the goal of building others up and reflecting God's redemptive love, not proving yourself right.

Can you think of a time when you misjudged someone's motives? How might empathy have changed your perspective?

How can praying for discernment help you respond with compassion rather than criticism?

In what ways does staying kingdom-focused influence your ability to engage others with grace and truth?

John 2:24-25 | Philippians 1:9-10 | 1 Samuel 16:7

Day 29   John 20:19–22

Share Like Jesus

Breathing Life Into Others

After the resurrection of Jesus, his confused and frightened followers huddled in a locked room. Jesus appeared to them and did something personal and profound. He breathed on them- preparing them for the new life that was about to begin. The same breath that had brought creation into being at the beginning of time and gave new life to the crucified Rescuer and Ruler of the world was now offered to them as a foretaste of what would soon come.

Jesus had spoken of His relationship with the Father, and was now extending that divine communion to His friends. The divine- life giving essence in Jesus, would soon be an embodied, empowering presence that would strengthen and guide them. Jesus, through the Holy Spirit, promised the provision of the spiritual abundance necessary to carry the Good News into the world. He modeled the ultimate form of generosity, sharing the dynamic, life-giving presence of God Himself.

Beyond the Material

We often think of sharing in terms of material goods—money, food, or possessions. Jesus certainly demonstrated generosity in those ways (like feeding the crowds with a few loaves and fish), And His life also pointed toward a deeper, more transformative sharing. By breathing the Holy Spirit over His disciples, He showed that sharing involves passing on spiritual gifts, hope, and divine relationship.

To share like Jesus means to trust that what we've received from God isn't meant to be hoarded—it's meant to be distributed. It's letting others share in our inheritance as children of God. Jesus didn't ration out the Holy Spirit based on merit or perfection. He promised the fullness of God's presence to men who had just recently scattered in fear.

When we share, we do so not from a place of scarcity, but from the abundance God has given. Everything God entrusts to us—whether physical, emotional, or spiritual—is not meant solely for our benefit. From the bread that feeds a crowd to the breath that imparts the Spirit, we're invited to hold all gifts with open hands, allowing God's abundance to flow through us.

How Now?

Identify Your Abundance: How can you share the more intangible gift (like faith, wisdom and empathy) God has entrusted to you?

Offer Encouragement and Guidance: Jesus gave the Spirit to encourage and empower His followers, look for opportunities to support others spiritually, praying for them, listening, and offering counsel.

Trust God's Provision: The fear of losing what we share often holds us back. Remember Jesus' example—He gave freely, confident in God's limitless resources.

What spiritual or relational gifts have you received that you can share?

What fears keep you from sharing generously, and how can Jesus' example help you overcome them?

Who in your life might need a reminder of God's abundance, and how can you share that with them?

Acts 2:1-4 | Romans 8:16-17 | 2 Corinthians 9:8

Day 30   Personal Reflection

Luke 14:1-23

One Sabbath, Jesus went to eat at the home of a prominent religious leader. The Sabbath was a holy and separate day, a time set apart for rest and worship when most Jews limited energy and activity to honor God. People were watching Him closely, curious about what He would say or do. A man with swollen arms and legs was there, and Jesus asked the group, "Is it permitted to heal on the Sabbath or not?" No one answered. So Jesus healed the man and sent him on his way. Then He turned to them and said, "If your child or even your ox fell into a well on the Sabbath, wouldn't you pull them out?" Again, they had nothing to say.

Jesus noticed how the guests picked the best seats at the table, so He told them a story:

"When you're invited to a wedding feast, don't grab the seat of honor. What if someone more important than you is invited? The host will ask you to move, and you'll be embarrassed in front of everyone. Instead, take the lowest seat. Then the host may come to you and say, 'Friend, move up to a better place.' You'll be honored in front of everyone. For those who lift themselves up will be brought down, and those who humble themselves will be lifted up."

Then Jesus turned to the host. "When you throw a dinner, don't just invite your friends, family, or rich neighbors. They might invite you back, and that would be your only reward. Instead, invite the poor, the disabled, the outcasts. You'll be blessed because they can't repay you, but God will reward you at the resurrection of the righteous."

Hearing this, someone at the table said, "Blessed is the one who will eat at the feast in God's kingdom."

Jesus responded with another story:

"A man prepared a great banquet and invited many guests. When everything was ready, he sent his servant to tell the guests, 'Come, everything is prepared.' But they all began to make excuses. One said, 'I just bought a field and need to go see it.' Another said, 'I just bought five pairs of oxen and need to try them out.' Another said, 'I just got married, so I can't come.'

"The servant returned and reported this to his master. The master became angry and said, 'Go quickly into the streets and alleys of the town. Bring in the poor, the disabled, the blind, and the lame.'

"The servant did as told but reported, 'There is still room.'

"The master said, 'Go out to the country roads and lanes. Compel everyone you find to come so my house will be full. I tell you, not one of those who were originally invited will get a taste of my banquet.'"

What about this encounter relates to your own life? What aspects of who Jesus connects to what it means to be human?

What actions does this story inspire you to take?

Day 31   Matthew 6:7–13

Pray Like Jesus

A Simple and Transformative Model

Throughout history, countless teachers and writers have reflected on Jesus' prayer life. Sometimes, the best way to learn is to return to the simplicity of how Jesus taught His disciples to pray. In first-century Judaism, it wasn't unusual for a rabbi- a teacher- to give their followers a set prayer. But when Jesus' disciples asked, *"Lord, teach us to pray,"* they weren't just seeking words—they longed for the profound connection they saw between Him and the Father.

Jesus' response, what we call the Lord's Prayer, is remarkable for both its brevity and depth. The disciples may have hoped for a secret "formula" to ensure their prayers were heard and answered- what Jesus offered were words that reveal God's character, reorient our hearts toward His kingdom, and remind us of our place in the divine story. To pray like Jesus helps us recognize our need for forgiveness and guidance, and understanding that prayer shapes us as much as it shapes the world around us.

Simplicity, Memorability, and Balance

Simplicity: Jesus warned against lengthy, showy prayers aimed at impressing others. His model is concise, yet it encompasses reverence for God, daily needs, forgiveness, and spiritual guidance.

Memorability: The Lord's Prayer is designed to be remembered and repeated. When words fail or our minds wander, it serves as a steady compass—easy to carry with us anywhere.

Balance: The prayer addresses three essential areas:

- Who God is: A loving Father, holy and set apart.
- What we need: Daily provision, forgiveness, and deliverance from evil.
- Our role in the world: Aligning with God's kingdom and extending His harmony to our relationships with others.

By praying this way, we learn to trust God with every aspect of our lives, to hold our requests in the light of His goodness, and to see prayer as not just a tool for changing circumstances, but for transforming our hearts.

How Now?

Pray Often: Jesus's prayer makes it easy to pray whenever and wherever we are.

Use Jesus' Words: Pray it word-for-word or use its themes as prompts. For example, "Your kingdom come" can lead you to pray for God's guidance and justice in specific situations.

Keep it Simple: Fancy words aren't required. God honors sincerity over eloquence.

Pray in Trust: Prayer is an act of dependency and faith—trusting God for daily bread and deliverance from evil.

Which part of the Lord's Prayer resonates most with your current season?

What simple adjustments can you make this week to bring your prayer life closer to Jesus' example of humility, trust, and alignment with the Father?

How might praying this way help you see God's work in your life and the world more clearly?

Philippians 4:6 | Luke 11:1 | Mark 1:35

Day 32 · John 4:39-42

Linger Like Jesus

Jesus Lingers in Samaria

The Samaritan woman ran into her village, her words tumbling out in breathless wonder: "Come, see a man who told me everything I ever did. Could He be the Messiah-The one who came to rescue the world?" Her urgency and astonishment stirred something in the hearts of her neighbors. They hurried to see this man she spoke of—Jesus, a Jewish rabbi at a well in Samaria, of all places.

When they arrived, they found Him receptive to their curiosity and eager to share the kingdom of God. The townspeople begged Him to stay, to linger in their community, and Jesus said yes. For two days, He shared meals, engaged in meaningful conversations, and taught about the love of the Father.

This wasn't just a casual detour. For a Jewish teacher to stay in Samaria, accepting hospitality from people His culture shunned, was radical. Jesus stayed, affirming their value and meeting their spiritual hunger. By the time He left, the villagers declared, "We no longer believe just because of what the women said; we have heard for ourselves, and we know that this man truly is the Rescuer"

Creating Space for Connection

Jesus' willingness to linger wasn't a sign of aimlessness—it was deeply intentional. He recognized the receptivity of the villagers and invested His time where hearts were open. Lingering creates opportunities for connection, trust, and transformation. It's a rhythm that allows kingdom values to take root in ways that hurried interactions never can.

Urgency often blinds us to opportunities to linger. We avoid slowing down for fear of overstaying or losing control of our schedules. Jesus shows us that honoring invitations and staying a little longer can foster profound relational depth. Open homes lead to open hearts. Being fully present shows others that they matter—not just for a moment, but in the broader story God is writing.

Lingering isn't about taking advantage of someone's hospitality or ignoring boundaries. It's about noticing when others extend an invitation to stay—spoken or unspoken—and reciprocating that welcome with our time and attention. Like Jesus, we can create space for relationships to move beyond surface interactions, allowing the seeds of the kingdom to grow.

How Now?

Recognize Invitations: Pay attention to when and where you are welcomed and valued. Invest your time where receptivity is clear.

Honor Hospitality: When someone invites you to linger— whether for a conversation, a meal, or shared time—accept their invitation with gratitude.

Engage Deeply: Prioritize quality interactions over rushing to the next task. Use the time you spend lingering to reflect God's love, encourage others, and invite transformation.

What practices or mindsets keep you from lingering with others? How can you let go of unnecessary urgency?

How might lingering create opportunities to reflect kingdom values in your relationships?

Luke 19:5-6 | Proverbs 27:17 | Ecclesiastes 3:1

Day 33   Matthew 15:21–28

Focus Like Jesus

Steadfast and Discerning

As Jesus traveled through regions with long-standing hostility toward Israel, a Canaanite woman approached Him with an urgent plea: her daughter was suffering terribly, and she desperately needed Jesus to act. His initial response was striking: *"I was sent only to the lost sheep of Israel."* At face value, these words might seem harsh or exclusive, as though Jesus were drawing a hard line. But what if He was voicing the divine mandate guiding His mission?

Jesus' primary calling was to Israel, God's chosen people, and He stayed focused on that task. He didn't chase every opportunity or yield to every voice demanding His attention. The encounter didn't end there. Moved by the woman's persistent faith, Jesus chose to step beyond His initial priority and heal her daughter. This moment illustrates a focus that wasn't rigid, but discerning—Jesus knew His calling, yet remained open to God's wider purposes as faith and need revealed themselves.

Focus With Flexibility

Staying focused on the direction God gives us can sometimes be misunderstood by others. Declining opportunities or narrowing our scope might seem uncaring or rigid. Yet, like Jesus, we must discern what God is asking of us and set boundaries accordingly. It's not that every other path is wrong—it's simply not what we're called to in this season.

Focus doesn't mean closing our hearts. Jesus models a non-rigid determination. He wasn't swayed by every request, nor did He dismiss genuine faith and need. His example shows us how to hold steady to our core mission while remaining flexible, gracious, and responsive when God's Spirit reveals unexpected opportunities.

How Now?

Know Your Core Calling: Clarify your sense of purpose and the specific people, tasks, or projects God has entrusted to you. Let this calling shape your decisions to say "yes" or "no."

Set Boundaries Without Apology: Don't feel guilty for declining good opportunities that are out of alignment with your current mission. True focus often requires saying "no."

Remain Open to Faith and Need: Stay attentive to moments when someone's genuine faith or need signals that God is inviting you to respond beyond your usual scope.

Embrace Misunderstanding: Understand that others may not always appreciate your boundaries. Stay humble and compassionate, trusting that faithfulness to God's direction will bear fruit in time.

What are the core elements of the mission God has placed before you?

Where do you struggle to say "no," and how might clarity about your calling help you make better decisions?

How can you balance staying true to your mission while remaining open to God's surprising purposes?

John 6:15 | Ephesians 5:15–17 | Proverbs 4:25–27

Day 34 · Mark 9:14–29

Battle Like Jesus

When Prayer and Fasting Are the Only Way

The disciples were stuck—exhausted from battling a force they couldn't overcome. A young man, tormented by a persistent evil spirit, lay beyond their ability to help. When Jesus arrived, the disciples explained their fruitless attempts, perhaps feeling defeated as Jesus effortlessly restored the boy.

Afterward, Jesus revealed the source of their struggle—and their lack of success: *"This kind can only come out by prayer and fasting."* The disciples had relied on physical effort and mental determination to face what required spiritual power. Jesus showed them a deeper truth: some battles can only be won through spiritual discipline.

Engaging in Spiritual Battle with Spiritual Tools

We live in a world where forces of evil—oppression, addiction, injustice—are painfully obvious. While we may hesitate to name them as spiritual forces, their grip on humanity is undeniable. Too often, we try to confront these struggles with sheer willpower, action plans, or last-ditch prayers for God to intervene. Jesus teaches us that certain battles demand we go deeper, leaning into the disciplines of prayer and fasting.

Prayer and fasting are not about magical solutions; they are about connection. Prayer aligns us with God's heart, drawing on His power rather than our own. Fasting disrupts our reliance on the physical, sharpening our spiritual focus. Together, these practices create space for God's Spirit to work in ways we cannot achieve on our own.

These disciplines also reflect the humility Jesus emphasized— done not for public recognition but in quiet intimacy with the Father (*Matthew 6*). They remind us that victory in spiritual battles isn't about the strength of our faith or will but the strength of our connection with God.

How Now?

Engage in Fasting with Intent: Consider fasting from food, media, or another regular comfort to heighten your dependence on God. Let the absence point you toward Him.

Pray with Specificity: Rather than offering generic prayers, ask God for wisdom and power in a specific battle you or others are facing.

Prepare for Long Battles: Spiritual battles often require persistence. Commit to ongoing prayer and fasting, trusting in God's timing and power.

Be Watchful, Not Fearful: Acknowledge the reality of spiritual forces without being consumed by fear. Rest in the authority of Christ, who has already overcome the powers of darkness.

What challenges in your life or community feel overwhelming?

How can incorporating fasting into your spiritual practices deepen your connection with God in these battles?

How can you maintain trust in God's power when answers to prayer seem delayed or unclear?

Ephesians 6:10–18 | Isaiah 58:6 | 2 Chronicles 20:3–4

Day 35 — John 13:1–17

Make Room Like Jesus

Creating Space

Jesus knew. He knew Judas would betray Him, and yet He didn't dismiss him or cast him out. At the Last Supper, a moment so sacred it would define generations of believers, Jesus knelt and washed Judas' feet—the betrayer's feet. He shared bread with him, meeting his gaze across the table.

This act wasn't passive acceptance of Judas' choices, nor was it resignation. It was an extension of grace—an accommodation to Judas' flaws and brokenness, creating one more opportunity for him to turn toward truth. Jesus made room for Judas, not by ignoring his sin but by choosing kindness and tolerance that invited repentance.

Jesus often made space for others to wrestle with their doubts, weaknesses, or misconceptions. He patiently explained His parables, answered Pharisees' testing questions, and even accommodated Thomas' skepticism after the resurrection. At every turn, Jesus met people where they were, refusing coercion or manipulation, instead inviting them to see and understand who He was.

The Strength of Kindness

To meet people where they are isn't a sign of weakness or compromise; it's a mark of strength. Jesus' tolerance wasn't about affirming every behavior or belief—it was about grace in action. It reflected the truth of Paul's words: *"It is God's kindness that leads to repentance"* (Romans 2:4).

Accommodating like Jesus doesn't mean approving what's harmful or wrong. It means creating space for growth, transformation, and relationship. It means sitting across from people whose choices or beliefs challenge us and choosing love over judgment. It's a posture of humility, holding the tension of grace and truth while trusting God to do the work of change.

Strongly held beliefs and convictions may tempt us to correct or control others, to force them to see things our way. Jesus shows us a better way: to offer patience, understanding, and room for others to encounter God's love on their own terms. This is the essence of accommodation—starting where people are, and walking with them toward where God is calling them to be.

How Now?

Extend Grace in Conflict: The next time you're tempted to correct or criticize, pause and consider how you can create space for understanding instead.

Practice Patience: Meeting people where they are takes time. Resist the urge to rush the process or demand immediate change.

Lead with Kindness: Acts of kindness and humility—not forceful arguments— open hearts and minds.

Trust God's Work: Accommodating others doesn't mean you're responsible for their transformation. Trust God to do the work in His timing.

Who in your life challenges your ability to extend grace? How can you make space for them without compromising your values?

How does Jesus' interaction with Judas shift your perspective on what it means to meet people where they are?

What might it look like to prioritize kindness over correction in your relationships?

Romans 2:4 | Psalm 103:8–10 | Matthew 5:43–48

Day 36 — Luke 4:16–21

Imagine Like Jesus

Vision of a Kingdom Breaking In

In the synagogue of His hometown, Jesus unrolled the scroll of Isaiah and read aloud words that painted a vivid picture: freedom for captives, sight for the blind, release for the oppressed, and good news for the poor. These weren't distant hopes—they were realities Jesus envisioned breaking into the present.

When He declared, *"Today this Scripture is fulfilled in your hearing,"* Jesus invited His listeners into His own imagination of the kingdom. It wasn't an abstract ideal but a tangible vision of restoration that guided everything He said and did. His parables expanded minds to see the kingdom of God through ordinary seeds, lost coins, and rebellious sons. His actions—touching the untouchable, dining with outcasts, and healing the broken—were manifestations of the kingdom He envisioned.

Seeing Possibilities

Jesus didn't just dream of God's reign; He lived it. His imagination bridged the gap between heaven and earth, offering a kingdom where the last are first, enemies are reconciled, and peace reigns. This wasn't escapism; it was the boldest form of engagement, shaping how He spoke, acted, and loved.

When we engage our imagination like Jesus, we begin to see our lives and communities through the lens of God's kingdom. Imagine Jesus' presence in your daily struggles. Picture Him in places of brokenness, bringing healing and hope. Visualize a world where forgiveness replaces resentment, where generosity overrides greed, and where every person is seen as an image-bearer of God. Let your imagination reach into the kingdom and build a bridge to your current reality.

To imagine like Jesus is to see the world not just as it is, but as it could be under God's rule. Imagination is an act of faith—it allows us to glimpse what is possible and align our actions with the vision of God's kingdom. Like Jesus, we can cultivate a holy imagination that turns divine promises into lived realities.

How Now?

Reflect on Jesus' Vision: Meditate on how Jesus described and demonstrated the kingdom of God. Let these images shape your prayers and actions.

Imagine Jesus' Presence: In moments of conflict or need, picture Jesus standing with you. How does His presence shift your perspective?

Tell Kingdom Stories: Like Jesus, use storytelling to spark imagination in others. Share parables, analogies, or personal experiences that reflect God's kingdom values.

Turn Vision Into Action: Let the kingdom you imagine inspire tangible steps to bring peace, justice, and love into your daily life.

How does imagining the kingdom of God change the way you approach challenges or relationships?

What aspects of Jesus' vision of the kingdom resonate most with you?

How can you use your imagination to align your actions with God's redemptive work in the world?

Matthew 13:31–33 | Ecclesiastes 3:11 | Isaiah 61:1–3

Day 37　　　　　　　　　　　　　　　　　　Matthew 19:13–15

Play Like Jesus

Interruptions That Bring Joy

Jesus was teaching one day, sharing insights with the gathered crowd and His disciples. A ruckus broke through the moment—children bursting onto the scene, their laughter and voices rising above the hum of adult conversation. To the disciples, this was an unwelcome interruption, a noisy distraction from the serious matters at hand. To Jesus, these children were no bother at all. He didn't wave them off or correct them for interrupting. Instead, He beckoned them closer.

Imagine these little ones—arms raised in anticipation, hoping to be lifted, spun around, or drawn into a playful chase. Children long to be seen, heard, and included. They want to share their stories, show off their discoveries, and simply enjoy being near someone who delights in them. Jesus welcomed them wholeheartedly. He paused His agenda, lowered Himself to their level, and embraced their spontaneous joy. In doing so, He gave us a glimpse of a kingdom where delight is celebrated, interruptions can be holy, and laughter flows freely.

Joyful Presence

We can see "fun" as an afterthought in our spiritual lives, something reserved for when work is done or obstacles are overcome. But Jesus shows us that the kingdom of God isn't only about solemn or "important" business—it's brimming with moments of lightness, humor, and delight. Children naturally understand this; they know how to find joy in the simplest things and value presence over productivity.

Jesus—the visible image of God—validated their desire to connect, play, and share their wonder. How interruptible are we when life hands us an opportunity for joy or playfulness? How often are we too busy, dignified, or serious to pause and embrace laughter or curiosity?

The children who ran to Jesus didn't worry about adult priorities or schedules; they just wanted to be close. And Jesus didn't scold them for their poor timing. He welcomed them, affirming that the kingdom of God has plenty of room for some silliness, spontaneity, and joy.

How Now?

Be Interruptible: The next time a child—or anyone—pulls you toward something joyful or unexpected, consider pausing instead of pushing them away.

Value Playfulness: Incorporate moments of fun into your daily rhythms. Allow yourself to laugh, explore, and delight in life's small wonders.

Embrace Presence Over Productivity: Recognize that being fully present with someone—especially a child—often matters more than sticking to a rigid schedule.

How can you welcome more playfulness and spontaneity into your life?

How might embracing joyful interruptions change your relationships or spiritual perspective?

What's one simple way you can show someone, young or old, that they are seen, heard, and valued today?

Psalm 126:2 | Philippians 4:4 | Ecclesiastes 3:4

Day 38   Luke 4:16–30

Unafraid Like Jesus

Moving Through Opposition

In His hometown of Nazareth, Jesus stood in the synagogue and read from the prophet Isaiah. At first, His words impressed the listeners, but when He suggested that God's mercy extended beyond their familiar boundaries and biases, admiration turned to outrage. The crowd, consumed by anger and offended pride, dragged Jesus to the edge of a cliff, determined to hurl Him into the void.

It's a chilling scene—fury unleashed in a moment of collective madness. Yet, as hostility surged, Jesus didn't cower or plead for mercy. Nor did He lash out or argue to defend Himself. Instead, He did something simple and bold: He walked through them. Jesus passed directly through the mob, looking them in the eye, brushing past their shoulders, and continued on His way.

In that tense standoff, Jesus showed that you can face opposition without losing your direction or dignity. He carried on in His mission, refusing to let their threats define or derail Him.

Facing Resistance Without Losing Purpose

Most of us will never face a crowd ready to throw us off a cliff, but we all encounter moments when living out kingdom values sparks opposition. Sometimes people respond to truth or faith-informed decisions with suspicion, pushback, or attempts to undermine us.

Jesus models a way forward that isn't passive silence or aggressive confrontation. It's a calm, purposeful movement. He walked through the chaos, head held high, anchored in His mission and identity. Hostility didn't deter Him or stick to His soul. Instead, He kept going—focused on God's calling and grounded in His Father's presence.

We too can learn to "walk through" the resistance we face—not by ignoring reality, but by refusing to let fear or rage reshape our purpose. This kind of quiet confidence flows from knowing who we are, what God has called us to do, and trusting in the One who walks with us.

Moving through life unafraid means continuing your journey even when anger, confusion, or resistance confronts you. It's about holding fast to truth, trusting God's strength, and moving forward with quiet confidence—no matter what pressures try to force you off course.

How Now?

Know Your Calling: Clarify your values and mission before opposition arises. When you're rooted in God's direction, you'll be less likely to fold under pressure.

Maintain Composure: Instead of reacting with anger or defensiveness, choose measured responses. Sometimes the most powerful answer is to keep moving forward with quiet resolve.

Trust God's Timing: Just as Jesus walked through the crowd, trust that God will guide you through tense circumstances. Stay aligned with His purpose, believing He'll make a way.

Recall a time when standing for what's right caused backlash or misunderstanding. How did you respond?

What fears hold you back from moving forward when others challenge your convictions?

How can you cultivate the calm confidence to walk through resistance without losing your footing or your faith?

John 2:24–25 | Psalm 27:1 | Isaiah 41:10

Day 39   Luke 23:32–34

Forgive Like Jesus

Mercy in the Midst of Cruelty

The actions that transpired at the top of a hill outside the city of Jerusalem was brutally unjust. Jesus, the so-called savior, hung suspended by nails, struggling for breath. Around Him, people mocked and sneered, soldiers gambled for His garments, and religious leaders relished the spectacle of His humiliation. The compassion of Jesus was met with inhuman cruelty.

In that moment of pain and betrayal, Jesus spoke words that shifted the axis of history: *"Father, forgive them, for they do not know what they are doing."* He chose mercy in the face of hate. He prayed for those killing Him. Rather than calling down wrath or seeking revenge, He offered what none of them deserved—grace.

The Hard, Holy Work of Forgiveness

Of all the" like Jesus" actions we can take, forgiveness is perhaps the most daunting- and likely the act that most helps us align our hearts with the heart of God. Forgiveness can feel impossible when wounds run deep and injustice glares us in the face. Without Jesus, forgiveness is nearly impossible. And Jesus didn't just talk about forgiveness; He lived it, modeling a mercy so radical it defies comprehension.

Jesus' forgiveness at the cross wasn't an endorsement of wrongdoing or passivity. It was a deliberate refusal to let vengeance or bitterness define reality. Forgiveness breaks the cycle of harm and grants freedom from the prison of resentment.

How did Jesus extend such profound forgiveness? His words—*"they do not know what they are doing"*—acknowledged that those who hurt Him acted out of ignorance, fear, and brokenness. Often, those who wound us are operating out of pain they don't even comprehend.

The journey toward forgiveness is sparked through empathy. It helps us see the human frailty behind harmful actions. It's a lifelong work, requiring repeated acts of re-living and responding. Jesus' model and commands to forgive invite us to lean into mercy continually, even when it feels unnatural. Prayer, empathy, and the Spirit's guidance will eventually reshape our hearts, making room for grace to flow.

How Now?

Begin with Prayer: When forgiveness feels unreachable, ask God for the willingness to start. He can slowly soften your heart.

Practice Empathy: Try to understand the woundedness behind another's hurtful actions.

Set Boundaries Wisely: Forgiveness doesn't mean tolerating abuse. We can release resentment without enabling harmful behavior.

Keep Trying: Forgiveness often involves continual practice. Each time bitterness surfaces, ask God to help you release it again.

Who are you struggling to forgive, and what small step can you take toward empathy and release?

How does Jesus' prayer from the cross challenge your understanding of what true forgiveness involves?

In what areas do you need to receive God's forgiveness for yourself, allowing that grace to strengthen your capacity to forgive others?

Matthew 18:21-22 | Colossians 3:13 | Genesis 50:20-21

Day 40   Revelation 5:6–10

Overcome Like Jesus

The Triumph of the Slain Lamb

The vision was overwhelming. John stood in awe, watching as a sealed scroll rested in God's hand. The scroll held the unfolding plan for redemption, but no one in heaven, on earth, or below the earth was found worthy to open it. Overcome with despair, John wept.

Then one of the elders spoke with reassurance: *"Do not weep! See, the Lion of the tribe of Judah, the Root of David, has triumphed. He is able to open the scroll."* John turned, expecting to see a mighty lion, regal and strong. Instead, he saw a Lamb, standing as though slain. The Lamb bore the marks of sacrifice—wounds from His suffering and death—but stood alive, triumphant, and at the center of God's throne.

All of heaven fell before Him- and a song rang out- *"Worthy is the Lamb who was slain, to receive power and wealth and wisdom and strength and honor and glory and praise!"*

In this moment, John saw the fullness of who Jesus is: the Lamb who overcame through sacrifice. His scars were not hidden or erased; they were glorified, a reminder of the suffering He endured for humanity and the victory He achieved through His resurrection.

Scars Transformed by Resurrection

Jesus' scars tell the story of His love. Even now, Christ carries the marks of His earthly suffering, showing that His humanity is not forgotten. These wounds, transformed by His resurrection, are no longer signs of pain but of victory, honor, and love.

We, too, carry scars—wounds inflicted by a fallen world, by others, and sometimes even by ourselves. Following Jesus means learning to embrace these scars, not as marks of shame but as the story of God's work in our lives. Through Christ, our wounds can be healed, our suffering can find purpose, and our scars can become reminders of His redemptive love.

To follow Jesus is to suffer and die to self, but it is also to rise with Him. The promise of the resurrection assures us that no wound inflicted upon us can separate us from God's love. Instead, these scars become a canvas where His grace is displayed.

How Now?

See Scars as Stories of Redemption: Reflect on how your wounds and scars testify to God's faithfulness and healing in your life.

Trust God's Healing Process: Healing doesn't erase the past; it transforms it. Invite God into your pain and let His love restore you.

Suffer with Purpose: Embrace the cost of discipleship, trusting that God can use your suffering to shape and grow you.

Find Hope in Resurrection: Just as Jesus' wounds were glorified, so too can your scars be redeemed and used for His purposes.

What scars—visible or hidden—do you carry, and how might they testify to God's work in your life?

How does seeing Jesus as both triumphant and wounded change the way you approach Him in prayer?

In what ways does the promise of resurrection give you hope, even in the midst of suffering?

Isaiah 53:5 | 2 Corinthians 12:9–10 | Philippians 3:10–11

Final Thoughts: The Journey Continues

I hope the words in this devotional alongside your reflections have increased your awareness of how striving to be like Jesus is profoundly simple and deeply challenging. To be like Jesus requires more than creating habits like quiet times and reflection—it demands intentionality, humility, and a willingness to let God shape every part of your life.

Along this journey, perhaps you've felt the tension Paul described when he admitted, "Not that I have already obtained all this, or have already arrived at my goal..." (Philippians 3:12). That realization isn't a failure—it's maturity. Recognizing how far we have to grow is a sign that we're on the right path.

This journey isn't meant to be walked alone. Becoming like Jesus happens in community, alongside others who are striving and stumbling toward the same goal. My hope is that you'll use this devotional not just to deepen your own faith but to extend it outward. Seek someone who can mentor you—a guide who's a few steps ahead. And in turn, reach back to someone who's searching, someone who needs encouragement to follow Jesus.

I also hope this devotional isn't a one-time experience. My prayer is that you'll return to these entries, whether for fresh perspective or renewed reflection, and that these words will continue to challenge and inspire you. If there are still blank pages, fill them. If you've already filled them, revisit them to see how you've grown.

The heart behind this work is to make the life and teachings of Jesus tangible. In a world where faith often feels complex or contentious, my deepest conviction is that embodying the ways of Jesus can renew us and spark a movement of love and grace. My challenge to you is simple: share this experience. Share it with someone who feels disconnected from God or someone who's hesitant to embrace faith. Be the bridge that invites them to encounter Jesus.

May the work of becoming more like Jesus never be finished. WIth every step, may you discover more of the person God created you to be. May all of us keep walking, keep reflecting, and keep sharing.

Like Jesus Prayer

Father,
Shape my heart to love like Jesus,
Open my eyes to see like Jesus,
Strengthen my hands to serve like Jesus,
And guide my steps to walk with Jesus.
Amen.

Appendix

Chronological Checklist based on the scripture references provided at the top right of each daily entry. Each entry is formatted with a checkbox, the Day Title from the journal, and the associated scripture reference.

- ☐ **Day 1: Grow Like Jesus** – Luke 2:41-45
- ☐ **Day 14: Obey Like Jesus** – Matthew 3:13-17
- ☐ **Day 20: Personal Reflection** – Matthew 4:1-17
- ☐ **Day 19: Wait Like Jesus** – John 2:1-11
- ☐ **Day 5: Teach Like Jesus** – Matthew 13:34-35
- ☐ **Day 4: Heal Like Jesus** – Mark 5:1-20
- ☐ **Day 24: Walk Like Jesus** – Luke 24:13-32
- ☐ **Day 6: Remember Like Jesus** – Luke 24:13-35
- ☐ **Day 7: Retreat Like Jesus** – Mark 1:35
- ☐ **Day 8: Silent Like Jesus** – Mark 14:60-61
- ☐ **Day 9: Talk Like Jesus** – Luke 9:28-36
- ☐ **Day 3: Include Like Jesus** – Luke 10:38-42
- ☐ **Day 2: Serve Like Jesus** – Matthew 20:26
- ☐ **Day 17: Eat Like Jesus** – Luke 7:43
- ☐ **Day 28: See Like Jesus** – Luke 5:22
- ☐ **Day 27: Cook Like Jesus** – John 21:1-14
- ☐ **Day 22: Ask Like Jesus** – John 5:1-9
- ☐ **Day 11: Impartial Like Jesus** – Luke 8:1-3
- ☐ **Day 18: Sleep Like Jesus** – Matthew 8:23-27
- ☐ **Day 23: Cry Like Jesus** – Luke 19:41-42
- ☐ **Day 29: Share Like Jesus** – John 20:19-22
- ☐ **Day 12: Witness Like Jesus** – Mark 1:14-15

- ☐ **Day 13: Comfortable Like Jesus** – Luke 7:36-50
- ☐ **Day 26: Invest Like Jesus** – Luke 6:12-16
- ☐ **Day 30: Reflection** – Luke 14:1-23
- ☐ **Day 15: Celebrate Like Jesus** – Luke 10:17-20
- ☐ **Day 16: Work Like Jesus** – Luke 2:52
- ☐ **Day 10: Personal Reflection** – Mark 3:20-34
- ☐ **Day 31: Pray Like Jesus** – Matthew 6:7-13
- ☐ **Day 32: Linger Like Jesus** – John 4:39-42
- ☐ **Day 25: Worship Like Jesus** – Luke 4:16
- ☐ **Day 33: Focus Like Jesus** – Matthew 15:21-28
- ☐ **Day 35: Make Room Like Jesus** – John 13:1-17
- ☐ **Day 36: Imagine Like Jesus** – Luke 4:16-21
- ☐ **Day 34: Battle Like Jesus** – Mark 9:14-29
- ☐ **Day 21: Fight Like Jesus** – John 2:13-17
- ☐ **Day 37: Play Like Jesus** – Matthew 19:13-15
- ☐ **Day 38: Unafraid Like Jesus** – Luke 4:16-30
- ☐ **Day 39: Forgive Like Jesus** – Luke 23:32-34
- ☐ **Day 40: Overcome Like Jesus** – Revelation 5:6-10

Made in the USA
Monee, IL
30 March 2025